Teacher's Book

A RESOURCE FOR PLANNING AND TEACHING

Level K WOW! Wonder of Words

Senior Authors J. David Cooper, John J. Pikulski

Authors Kathryn H. Au, Margarita Calderón, Jacqueline C. Comas, Marjorie Y. Lipson, J. Sabrina Mims, Susan E. Page, Sheila W. Valencia, MaryEllen Vogt

Consultants Dolores Malcolm, Tina Saldivar, Shane Templeton

INVITATIONS TO LITERACY

W9-AUF-262

Houghton Mifflin Company • Boston

Atlanta • Dallas • Geneva, Illinois • Palo Alto • Princeton

Acknowledgments

Grateful acknowledgment is made for permission to reprint copyrighted material as follows:

ABC and You, by Eugenie Fernandes. Copyright © 1990 by Eugenie Fernandes. Reprinted by permission of Ladybird Books.

Faces, by Shelley Rotner and Ken Kreisler. Text copyright © 1994 by Shelley Rotner and Ken Kreisler. Photographs copyright © 1994 by Shelley Rotner. Reprinted by permission of Simon & Schuster Books for Young Readers, Simon & Schuster Children's Publishing Division.

"I Am Special, I Am Me," by Deborah K. Coyle, from *Everybody Sings,* compiled by Deborah K. Coyle. Copyright © 1991 by Deborah K. Coyle. Reprinted by permission of the Estate of Deborah K. Coyle.

Mr. Rabbit and the Lovely Present, by Charlotte Zolotow, illustrated by Maurice Sendak. Text copyright © 1962 by Charlotte Zolotow. Illustrations copyright © 1962 by Maurice Sendak. Reprinted by permission of HarperCollins Publishers.

My Big Dictionary, by the Editors of the American Heritage Dictionaries, illustrated by Pamela Cote. Copyright © 1994 by Houghton Mifflin Company. All rights reserved.

On Monday When It Rained, by Cherryl Kachenmeister, photographs by Tom Berthiaume. Copyright © 1989 by Cherryl Kachenmeister and Tom Berthiaume. Reprinted by permission of Houghton Mifflin Company. All rights reserved.

Rain, by Robert Kalan, illustrated by Donald Crews. Text copyright © 1978 by Robert Kalan. Illustrations copyright © 1978 by Donald Crews and Robert Kalan. Reprinted by permission of Greenwillow Books, a division of William Morrow & Company, Inc.

"Rain Song," from *Is Someplace Always Very Far Away?* revised edition, by Leland B. Jacobs. Copyright © 1993 by Allen D. Jacobs. Reprinted by permission of Henry Holt and Company, Inc.

"Reflection," from *Wide Awake and Other Poems,* by Myra Cohn Livingston. Copyright © 1959, renewed 1987 by Myra Cohn Livingston. Reprinted by permission of Marian Reiner for the author.

"Sing a Rainbow," by Arthur Hamilton, from *Pete Kelley's Blues.* Copyright © 1955 by Mark VII Music. Copyright renewed. All rights administered by WB Music Corp. All rights reserved. Reprinted by permission.

"What Is Pink?" by Christina Georgina Rossetti.

Who Said Red? by Mary Serfozo, illustrated by Keiko Narahashi. Text copyright © 1988 by Mary Serfozo. Illustrations copyright © 1988 by Keiko Narahashi. Reprinted by permission of Margaret K. McElderry Books, Simon & Schuster Children's Publishing Division.

Copyright © 1997 by Houghton Mifflin Company. All rights reserved.

Permission is hereby granted to teachers to reprint or photocopy in classroom quantities the pages or sheets in this work that carry a Houghton Mifflin Company copyright notice. These pages are designed to be reproduced by teachers for use in their classes with accompanying Houghton Mifflin materials, provided each copy made shows the copyright notice. Such copies may not be sold and further distribution is expressly prohibited. Except as authorized above, prior written permission must be obtained from Houghton Mifflin Company to reproduce or transmit this work or portions thereof in any other form or by any other electronic or mechanical means, including any information storage or retrieval system, unless expressly permitted by federal copyright law. Address inquiries to School Permissions, Houghton Mifflin Company, 222 Berkeley Street, Boston, MA 02116.

Printed in U.S.A.

ISBN: 0-395-79542-7

23456789-B-99 98 97

Photography Credits

THEME: All About Me

Dave Desroches, p. T55; Richard Haynes, pp. T27, T30; Tony Scarpetta, p. T51; Tracey Wheeler, pp. T13, T27, T29, T31, T33, T53, T55, T57, T58-T59, T83, T84-T85, T89, T91; Banta Digital Group, pp. T27, T31, T59, T81, T84, T91; Karen Ahola, pp. T28, T33; Cathy Copeland, pp. T26, T50, T58, T80-T81, T90; Eugenie Fernandes, p. T34; José Ramon Garcia, p. T60; Ken Kriestler, p. T60; Piotr Kaczmarek, p. T13

THEME: Color Is Everywhere

Karen Ahola, p. T148; Cathy Copeland, pp. T118-T119, T170; John Lei, pp. T109, T144; Richard Haynes, p. T141; Ken Karp, p. T180; Tony Scarpetta, pp. T149, T184; Tracey Wheeler, pp. T105, T121, T123, T125, T143, T145, T147, T149, T171, T173, T175, T178-T179, T180-T181; Banta Digital Group, pp. T118-T119, T120-T121, T122-T123, T124-T125, T129, T178; HarperCollins, p. T106; Simon and Schuster, p. T150, Piotr Kaczmarek, p. T105

All About Me

Table of Contents
THEME: All About Me

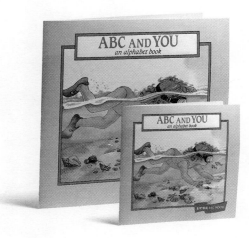

Big Book *LITERATURE FOR WHOLE CLASS AND SMALL GROUP INSTRUCTION*

by Shelley Rotner and Ken Kreisler
photographs by Shelley Rotner

nonfiction

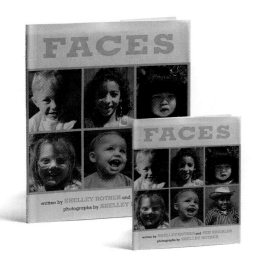

WATCH ME READ Book *PRACTICE FOR ORAL LANGUAGE AND STORYTELLING SKILLS*

Each title is also available in black and white. This version includes a home activity.

WATCH **ME** READ

First Day of School

Bibliography
Books for the Library Corner

 Multicultural

 Science/Health

 Math

 Social Studies

 Music

 Art

I Am an Explorer
by Amy Moses
Childrens 1990 (32p)
A boy imagines he is exploring the world while playing in the park.

I Like Books
by Anthony Brown
Knopf 1988 (24p)
A monkey describes the kinds of books he likes. **Available in Spanish as *Me gustan los libros.***

Just Like Me
by Barbara J. Neasi
Childrens 1984 (32p)
A girl describes what makes her different from her twin sister.
Available in Spanish as *Igual que yo.*

Make a Face: A Book with a Mirror
by Henry and Amy Schwartz
Scholastic 1994 (24p)
Children show different emotions with their facial expressions.

Kindergarten Kids
by Ellen B. Senisi
Scholastic 1994 (32p)
A kindergarten class talks about a typical day of work and play.

I Like Me
by Nancy Carlson
Puffin 1990 (32p)
A pig explains why she likes herself.

All I Am
by Eileen Roe
Bradbury 1990 (32p)
A young boy names the many things he is, including a friend, neighbor, and helper.

Sunshine
by Jan Ormerod
Morrow 1990 (32p) paper
A girl feeds and dresses herself when she awakens before her parents. (Wordless)

My Day: A Book in Two Languages /Mi día: Un libro en dos lenguas
by Rebecca Emberley
Little 1993 (32p)
A child's daily activities are described. **In English and Spanish.**

My Kitchen
by Harlow Rockwell
Greenwillow 1980 (24p)
A boy describes his kitchen and the meal being prepared for him.

My Food
illustrated by Lisa-Theresa Lenthall
Bantam 1994 (16p)
Names of foods are presented. **In English, Spanish, French, and German.**

Piggies
by Audrey and Don Wood
Harcourt 1991 (32p)
A child imagines ten piggies dancing on her fingers and toes.

Up and Up
by Shirley Hughes
Lothrop 1986 (32p)
A girl discovers a way to fly. (Wordless)

While I Am Little
by Heidi Goennel
Tambourine 1993 (32p)
A boy explains why he likes being young.

Books for Teacher Read Aloud

Hats Off to Hair!
by Virginia Kroll
Charlesbridge 1995 (32p)
A poetic tribute to all kinds of hair from cornrows and crew cuts to pigtails and spikes.

Andrew's Bath
by David McPhail
Little 1984 (32p)
Andrew fills his tub with imaginary friends while taking his first bath alone. **Available in Spanish as *El baño de Andrés.***

Honey, I Love
by Eloise Greenfield
Harper 1995 (20p)
This poem celebrates the everyday things a young girl loves.

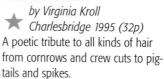

Grandmother's Chair
by Ann Herbert Scott
Clarion 1990 (32p)
A girl inherits the chair her mother, grandmother, and great-grandmother owned.

Hard to Be Six
by Arnold Adoff
Lothrop 1991 (32p)
A boy describes the difficulties of being six.

I've Got Chicken Pox
by True Kelley
Dutton 1994 (32p)
Jess is excited to have chicken pox but soon realizes that it's no fun to be sick.

Maxine in the Middle
by Holly Keller
Greenwillow 1989 (32p)
Maxine is fed up with being the middle child in her family.

Me and Neesie
by Eloise Greenfield
Crowell 1975 (40p) Harper 1984 paper
Janell won't give up her imaginary friend until she makes friends at school.

Mommy's Office
by Barbara Shook Hazen
Atheneum 1992 (32p)
Emily's day at her mother's office reminds her of her days at school.

My Mama Needs Me
⭐ *by Mildred Pitts Walter*
Lothrop 1983 (32p)
Jason is afraid his mother won't need him after his baby sister is born.

Rachel Parker, Kindergarten Show-Off
by Ann Martin
Holiday 1992 (32p) also paper
Olivia is jealous of Rachel, her new neighbor and classmate.

Some Days, Other Days
by P. J. Petersen
Scribners 1994 (32p)
Jimmy doesn't want to get up because he is afraid he will have a bad day.

When We Grow Up
by Anne Rockwell
Dutton 1982 (32p)
Classmates imagine themselves grown up and working at a variety of jobs.

Wilson Sat Alone
by Debra Hess
Simon 1994 (32p)
Wilson is too shy to join the activities of the children in his class.

Books for Shared Reading

Is That Josie?
⭐ *by Keiko Narahashi*
Macmillan 1994 (24p)
Josie imagines that she is all kinds of animals while playing with her mother.

Mama, Do You Love Me?
⭐ *by Barbara M. Joosse*
Chronicle 1991 (32p)
An Inuit child discovers her mother's love for her is unconditional.

My Shadow
by Robert Louis Stevenson
Putnam 1990 (32p)
A poem describes the fun a child has with his shadow.

I Am Six
⭐ *by Ann Morris*
Silver Press 1995 (32p)
In this photo essay, children sing, paint, read, count, and write their way through a day of school.

One, Two, Three, Count with Me
⬛ *by Catherine and Laurence Anholt*
Viking 1994 (24p)
A simple counting book explores elements familiar to young children.

Walk with Me
by Naomi Davis
Scholastic 1995 (24p)
A girl enjoys a walk to the park with her mother.

Dancing Feet
⭐ *by Charlotte Agell*
Gulliver 1994 (36p)
Children use their feet, hands, eyes, and other body parts in daily activities.

What Am I?
by Stephanie Calmenson
Harper 1989 (32p)
A collection of simple riddles.

Shouting Sharon: A Riotous Counting Rhyme
⬛ *by David Pace*
Golden 1995 (32p)
Sharon's shouting brings surprising results that almost get her into trouble.

Technology Resources

Computer Software

Internet See the Houghton Mifflin Internet resources for additional bibliographic entries and theme-related activities.

Video Cassettes

Arthur's Eyes *by Marc Brown.* Am. Sch. Pub.

Did I Ever Tell You How Lucky You Are? *by Dr. Seuss.* Listening Library

Just Me and My Dad *by Mercer Mayer.* Listening Library

My First Nature Video Filmic Archives

If I Ran the Zoo *by Dr. Seuss.* Am. Sch. Pub.

Audio Cassettes

Mommy's Office *by Barbara Shook Hazen.* Spoken Arts

It's Mine *by Leo Lionni.* Am. Sch. Pub.

I Am Not Going to Get Up Today *by James Stevenson.* Am. Sch. Pub.

Filmstrips

A Look at You: From Head to Toe; In Touch with Your Senses Nat'l Geo

I Like Me! *by Nancy Carlson.* Weston Woods

D.W. Flips! *by Marc Brown.* Am. Sch. Pub.

AV addresses are in the Teacher's Handbook, pages H15–H16.

Theme at a Glance

Reading/Listening Center

Selections	Comprehension Skills and Strategies	Phonemic Awareness	Concept Development	Concepts About Print
On Monday When It Rained	✔ Noting details, T19, T28 Faces and feelings!, T28 Reading strategies, T18, T20, T22, T24 **Rereading and responding,** T26–T27	✔ Rhyming words, T25, T29 Glad or sad game, T29 Rain, rain, go away!, T29		
ABC and You	✔ Sequence, T43, T52 Noting details, T45 Alphabetical order, T52 Reading strategies, T38, T42, T44, T46, T48 **Rereading and responding,** T50–T51		✔ Letter names, T49 Naming the capital letters, T53 Capital and small letters, T53 More with letter names, T53 Big A little a, T53	✔ Letter as letter, T39 What's a letter?, T54 Capital or small, T54 Names in print, T54
Faces	✔ Categorize and classify, T69, T82 Noting details in photographs, T82 Reading strategies, T64, T68, T72, T74, T76 **Rereading and responding,** T80–T81		Parts of the body, T75, T83 Name the feature, T83	✔ Book handling, T65 Where does a page begin and end?, T84 Right side up, T84 Where does a book begin and end?, T84

✔ *Indicates Tested Skills. See page T11 for assessment options.*

Language/Writing Center

Cross-Curricular Center

Listening	Oral Language	Writing	Content Areas
	Story week, T30 My own feelings, T30 Feelings ball, T30	Weather words, T31 My friends, T31 New toys for the sandbox, T31	**Math:** is Peter there, please?, T32; and Sunday makes seven, T32 **Art:** colors and feelings, T33 **Music:** mood music, T33
Listen and read, T55 Find the Letter, T55 Who am I describing?, T55	Talking about words, T56 Sharing experiences, T56 Where have we seen letters?, T56	Class story, T37 Writing the alphabet, T57 Feeling the ABCs, T57 Sentence strips, T57	**Creative Movement:** body letters, T58; name cheers, T58 **Art:** crayon rubbings, T59 **Math:** how many letters, T59
Following directions, T85 What do you hear?, T85 Listen and read, T85	Faces talking, T88 The telephone game, T88 What else can faces do? T88 Home connection, T88	Class story, T63 Sharing ideas, T87 Exploring letter forms, T87 Body diagrams, T89 My eyes are brown, T89 Me and my name, T89	**Math:** hearing patterns, T90; counting, T90 **Art:** look at me!, T90 **Social Studies:** costumes around the world, T91 **Science:** the five senses, T91

Meeting Individual Needs

Key to Meeting Individual Needs

 Students Acquiring English

Activities and notes throughout the lesson plans offer strategies to help children understand the selections and lessons.

 **Challenge**

Challenge activities and notes throughout the lesson plans suggest additional activities to stimulate critical and creative thinking.

 Extra Support

Activities and notes throughout the lesson plans offer additional strategies to help children experience success.

Managing Instruction

Whole-Class Instruction

For some of your instructional work, whole-class instruction is appropriate. Reading aloud to children, shared reading, and modeled writing are good whole-class activities. For other lessons, small flexible groups will be appropriate. If the content of the lesson will benefit everyone and the format will actively involve all children, use whole-class instruction. For whole-class activities, teachers often have children work in cooperative teams and engage children in drawing, writing, and working with concrete materials.

For further information on this and other Managing Instruction topics, see the *Professional Development Handbook.*

Performance Standards

During this theme, children will

- *discover that story characters are like them in many ways*
- *make predictions and evaluate them*
- *retell or summarize each selection*
- *learn about parts of the body*
- *apply comprehension skills: Noting Details, Sequence, Categorize/Classify*
- *recognize letter names*
- *recognize rhymes*
- *write a story*

Students Acquiring English	Challenge	Extra Support
• **Develop Key Concepts** Children focus on Key Concepts through playing word and letter games, making word webs and charts, and drawing self-portraits.	• **Apply Critical Thinking** Children apply critical thinking by making up stories that incorporate details, sequencing the alphabet, and categorizing and classifying.	• **Receive Increased Instructional Time on Skills** Practice activities in the Reading/Listening Center provide support with noting details, categorizing and classifying, and learning to follow sequence. Children also receive additional work on recognizing rhyming words and distinguishing between capital and lower-case letters.
• **Expand Vocabulary** Children use context and picture clues, discuss meanings, and model definitions. Children learn names for days of the week, words expressing emotions, and parts of the body.	• **Explore Real-life Situations** Activities that motivate further exploration include writing about interests, brainstorming games and learning about clothing from around the world.	
• **Act as a Resource** Children are asked to share their experiences by role-playing situations involving their feelings.	• **Engage in Creative Thinking** Opportunities for creative expression include drawing, body movement, and creating self-portrait masks.	• **Provide Independent Reading** Children choose to explore books and to read independently when exciting, theme-related literature is made available. (See Bibliography, T6–T7.)

Additional Resources

Invitaciones

Develop bi-literacy with this integrated reading/language arts program in Spanish. Provides authentic literature and real-world resources from Spanish-speaking cultures.

Language Support

Translations of Big Books in Chinese, Hmong, Khmer, and Vietnamese. *Teacher's Booklet* provides instructional support in English.

Students Acquiring English Handbook

Guidelines, strategies, and additional instruction for students acquiring English

Planning for Assessment

Informal Assessment

Observation Checklists

- Concepts About Print/Book Handling
- Responding to Literature and Decoding Behaviors and Strategies
- Writing Behaviors and Stages of Temporary Spelling
- Listening and Speaking Behaviors
- Story Retelling and Rereading

Literacy Activity Book

Recommended pages for children's portfolios:
- Recognizes Rhymes, p. 3
- Personal Response, p. 4
- Comprehension: Sequence, p. 7
- Language Patterns, p. 10
- Concept Development: Body Parts, p. 12

Retellings—Oral/Written

- *Teacher's Assessment Handbook*

Formal Assessment

Kindergarten Literacy Survey

Evaluates children's literacy development. Provides holistic indicator of children's ability with
- Shared Reading/Constructing Meaning
- Concepts About Print
- Phonemic Awareness
- Emergent Writing

Managing Assessment

Question How can I assess the emergent reading and writing of kindergarten children?

Answer In kindergarten, it is often difficult to assess children's progress using samples of their work. At this level, observations are often the most useful. Try these ideas:

- Establish a regular schedule and a place for recording your observations. Focus on only a few students each day. Some teachers keep their notes in a 3-ring notebook, using a separate page for each child. Others use recipe cards or mailing labels. Keeping separate pages for each child allows you to share notes with parents and allows you to expand as needed.

- Keep children's drawings and the writing that often accompanies them as evidence of emerging abilities—story sense, listening comprehension, concepts about print, letter recognition, and temporary spelling.

- Create opportunities for children to write for functional purposes. Many of these opportunities are included in the *Teacher's Book* for each theme. Look for other opportunities, such as creating menus, birthday cards, invitations, and picture captions.

- Audio tape retellings of a story the children have heard.

For more information on this and other topics, see the *Teacher's Assessment Handbook*.

Portfolio Assessment

The portfolio icon signals portfolio opportunities throughout the theme.

Additional Portfolio Tips:

- Introducing Portfolios to the Class, T93

Launching the Theme

See the Houghton Mifflin **Internet** resources for additional activities.

Song Tape for All About Me: *I Am Special, I Am Me*

INTERACTIVE LEARNING

Warm-Up

Singing the Theme Song

- Play the Song Tape "I Am Special, I Am Me" for children. (For lyrics see *Teacher's Handbook,* page H12.)

- Then play the song again, encouraging children to sing along.

- Show children the books for this theme, explaining that all of the books are about children, and just like the children in this class, each child is special.

Interactive Bulletin Board

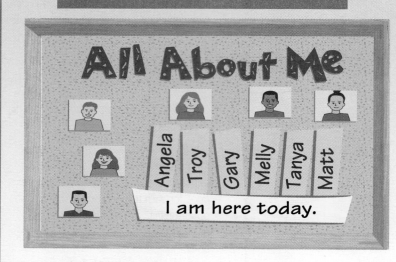

Look at Us

- Explain to children that as they learn about the children in the stories, they will also learn about each other.

- Take individual pictures of all the children in the class to put on the Theme Board. Label the pictures with name cards.

- Make a long pocket for the bottom of the Theme Board. Write on it: **I am here today.** Have children put their name cards in the pocket when they arrive in the morning.

See the *Home/Community Connections Booklet* for theme-related materials.

Portfolio Opportunity

The Portfolio Opportunity icon highlights portfolio opportunities throughout the theme.

Ongoing Project:

All About Me Book

Invite children to make a book about themselves.

- Make a blank book for each child.

- Begin by writing the following sentences on children's pages and having children illustrate them: My name is _____.; This is where I live.; Here are some people in my family.

Use opportunities throughout this theme for children to draw and write about themselves.

Choices for Centers

Creating Centers

Use these activities to create Learning Centers in the classroom.

Reading/Listening Center

- Faces and Feelings!, T28
- Sequencing Names, T52
- Categorize and Classify, T82

Language/Writing Center

- Feelings Ball, T30
- Talking About Words, T56
- Me and My Name, T89

Cross-Curricular Center

- Math: Is Peter There, Please?, T32
- Art: Crayon Rubbings, T59
- Social Studies: Costumes Around the World, T91

READ ALOUD

SELECTION:
On Monday When It Rained

by Cherryl Kachenmeister

Selection Summary

A young boy shares how his feelings change with each new day of a week.
On Monday, he is disappointed. On Tuesday, he is embarrassed. By Sunday
night, he wonders if all weeks are full of so many different emotions. Each
feeling is demonstrated through captivating photos of the boy.

Lesson Planning Guide

	Skill/Strategy Instruction	Meeting Individual Needs	Lesson Resources
1 Introduce *the* Literature *Pacing: 1 day*	**Preparing to Listen and Write** Warm-Up/Build Background, T16 Read Aloud, T16–T17	**Extra Support,** T16 **Choices for Rereading,** T17 **Students Acquiring English,** T17	**Poster** If You're Happy and You Know It *Literacy Activity Book* Personal Response, p. 1 **Story Props,** T17
2 Interact *with* Literature *Pacing: 1–2 days*	**Reading Strategies** Monitor, T18 Evaluate, T18, T20, T24 Self-Question, T20 Summarize, T22 **Minilessons** ✔ Noting Details, T19 ✔ Rhyming Words, T25	**Students Acquiring English,** T18, T22, T25, T26, T27 **Extra Support,** T18, T20, T23 **Challenge,** T19 **Rereading and Responding,** T26–T27	See the Houghton Mifflin, **Internet** resources for additional activities.
3 Instruct *and* Integrate *Pacing: 1–2 days*	**Reading/Listening Center** Comprehension, T28 Phonemic Awareness, T29 **Language/Writing Center** Oral Language, T30 Writing, T31 **Cross-Curricular Center** Cross-Curricular Activities, T32–T33	**Students Acquiring English,** T32 **Extra Support,** T28, T29, T32 **Challenge,** T28, T29, T33	**Poster** School Days **Letter, Word, and Picture Cards,** T32 *Literacy Activity Book* Comprehension, p. 2 Phonemic Awareness, p. 3 See the Houghton Mifflin **Internet** resources for additional activities.

✔ *Indicates Tested Skills. See page T11 for assessment options.*

1

Introduce *the* Literature

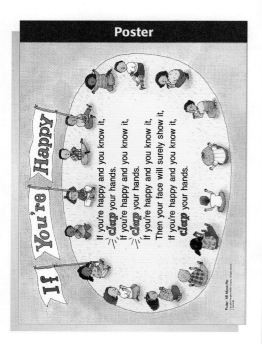

Poster

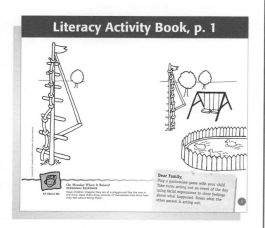

Literacy Activity Book, p. 1

Preparing to Listen and Write

Warm-Up/Build Background

Sharing a Song

- Display the poster for "If You're Happy and You Know It" and read or sing it for children. (See Teacher's Handbook, p. H10.)

- Ask children to name things that make them happy and what they do when they are feeling that way.

- Then invite the children to say or sing the song along with you as you go through it again.

Read Aloud

LAB, p.1

Preview and Predict

- Display the cover of *On Monday When it Rained.* Read the title and the author's and photographer's names.

- Tell children that in the story a boy tells about all his different feelings during a week. Ask them what the boy's face on the cover tells us about the way he is feeling about the rain on Monday. (He is unhappy.)

- Take a "picture walk" through page 13 of the story and ask children to look for and comment on other ways the boy is feeling . Then ask them to predict why the boy might be feeling these different ways and what other feelings he might have during the week.

Read

- Invite children to listen to the story to see if their predictions match what happens.

- As you read, pause from time to time to allow children to comment on the boy's feelings and to revise their predictions. Guide them to understand that the boy's different feelings are normal and part of an ordinary week in his life.

Extra Support You may also want to discuss the meanings of words that may be unfamiliar such as *disappointed, embarrassed,* and *proud.* In discussing the words, you might suggest other words that have almost the same meaning such as *sad* or *unhappy* for *disappointed.* Whenever available, use picture clues for vocabulary support.

Personal Response	**Home Connection** Invite children to talk about what they liked and disliked about the story. Then, have them complete *Literacy Activity Book,* page 1. Encourage children to take the page home to share with their families.

More Choices for Rereading

Rereadings provide varied, repeated experiences with the literature so that children can make its language and content their own. The following rereading choices appear on page T26.

- Likes and Dislikes
- Act It Out
- Timeline

Choices for Rereading

Vocabulary Expansion: Days of the Week

As you read, help children recognize the names for the days of the week that are found in the story. Ask them to raise their hands when they hear you say them. You might also take this opportunity to have children practice reciting the days of the week starting with Monday. Then reread the story encouraging children to chime in on the days of the week.

Students Acquiring English Encourage children who are learning English to teach other children the names for days of the week in their primary language. Also, post calendars in other languages for children to view. They are often available in ethnic restaurants.

Me Too!

As they listen, have children think of times they feel the way the boy in the story feels . Pause occasionally as you reread the story for children to tell about their experiences.

Frame the Face

Help children use the Story Retelling Prop frame to help them retell the story. Ask children to take turns acting the part of the boy in the story. As you read, have them hold the frame so it surrounds their faces. When they hear a feeling word, invite them to make a face which expresses it.

Materials
- Story Retelling Props (See Teacher's Handbook, page H2.)

Interact *with* Literature

On Monday when it rained
my mother said I couldn't play outside.

I wanted to ride
my new red bike with the blue horn
to my friend Maggie's house.

I was…

3

Disappointed

4

Reading Strategies

▶ **Monitor**
Evaluate

Teacher Modeling Explain to children that good readers do many things to help themselves enjoy and understand a story. Model for children how good readers think about how the words and the pictures go together.

Think Aloud

I remember that the boy in the story tells something that happened and then he tells how it made him feel. The pictures show how he felt. If I'm confused or don't understand any of his feelings, I'll pause to remember what he said happened and look closely at his face. I'll think about how I'd feel if it happened to me and if I 'd make the same face. If I do this, I'll understand his feelings and will enjoy the story more.

Purpose Setting

As you reread the story, pause at each picture and suggest that children think about how the boy felt and if they would feel the same way.

Students Acquiring English

These strategies encourage children to use picture clues and other cues and to draw on their personal experience.

Visual Literacy

Use pages 4 and 5 to point out the beginning of the story's text and picture pattern. The text on the left page tells how the boy feels; the photo on the right page shows how he feels.

MEETING INDIVIDUAL NEEDS **Extra Support**

Word Meaning Ask children how they would feel if they couldn't ride their bike to their friend's house. If necessary, restate their responses in a way that defines the word *disappointed*.

Science Link

Recall with children that the boy can't ride his bike because it's raining. Invite children to talk about other types of weather that might prevent them riding their bikes. *(snow, lightning, cold)*

On Tuesday when my grandma came to dinner
we had macaroni and cheese and chocolate milk.

I drank my chocolate milk real fast,
and right before we had the cookies for dessert
I burped out loud.

I was…

7

Embarrassed

8

Comprehension
Noting Details

Teach/Model

Read aloud pages 3 and 4 of *On Monday When It Rained,* asking children to listen carefully to find out what happens to make the boy feel disappointed. Show children how recalling the boy's words will help them.

Think Aloud

I listened carefully and I remember that the boy's mother wouldn't let him go outside because it was raining. I also remember that he wants to ride his bike to his friend's house. If I couldn't ride my bike to my friend's house, I'd be disappointed too!

Practice/Apply

Read aloud page 7. Ask children what helped them to know why the boy feels embarrassed.

SKILL FINDER
Noting Details, p. T28

Minilessons,
See Themes 3, 6, 7

Math Link

Invite children to tell you what time of day it is. If needed, review times of day with children (morning, afternoon, evening, night)

MEETING INDIVIDUAL NEEDS
Challenge

Noting Details Reread page 7 and challenge children to recall what the boy had for dinner. *(macaroni and cheese, chocolate milk, cookies for dessert)*

2

Interact with Literature

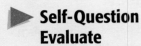

READ ALOUD

Reading Strategies

▶ **Self-Question**
Evaluate

Teacher Modeling Explain to children that careful readers ask themselves questions during a story to help understand and enjoy the story. Read pages 15–16 and then say:

Think Aloud

I know the boy was scared of the monster that was in the movie. So I ask myself, would I be scared of the monster in the movie? The words tell me that it was big and green with a long tail and scales. I can picture it in my mind. I think I would be scared too.

On Wednesday when I went to pre-school we drew pictures of big animals in a zoo.

My teacher, Laura, said my elephant looked just like one she saw at the zoo last summer.

I was...

11

Proud

12

QuickREFERENCE

Extra Support

To help children better understand how the boy feels, discuss how it would make them feel if someone said their drawing of something looked just like the real thing.

O n Thursday when I watched a movie
there was this one part where a big monster
ate a whole building.

My sister said that monsters aren't real,
but this one was green and had a long tail and scales
and it looked real to me.

I was…

15

Scared

16

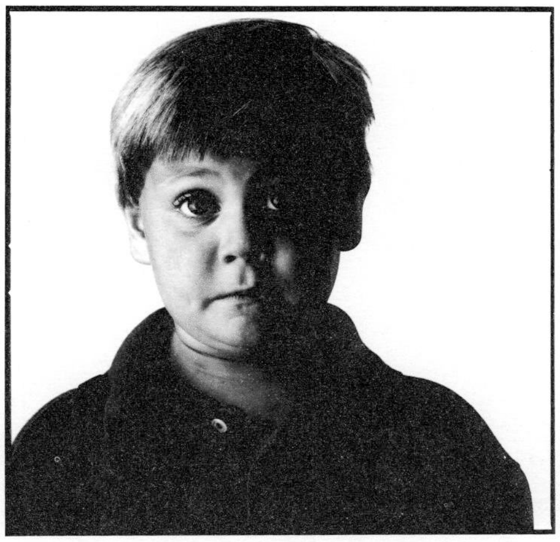

Journal

Have children draw the monster described on page 15 and dictate or write a sentence telling whether or not they would have been scared by it.

Interact *with* Literature

READ ALOUD

Reading Strategies

▶ **Summarize**

Teacher Modeling Tell children that good readers look for the important parts of a story to help them remember it. Model for children how to remember important information from a story.

Think Aloud

I want to remember the important things that happened in the story. I know that the story follows the order of the days of the week. If I think about the order of the days of a week and how the boy feels on each day, it will help me to remember what has happened so far in the story. Then I will continue reading to remember what happens at the end.

On Friday when I went to my cousin Janie's she wouldn't let me play with her new dump truck in the sandbox.

I always share my toys with her when she comes to my house and I have something new to play with.

I was...

19

Angry

20

QuickREFERENCE

Students Acquiring English

If children seem confused about why the child is angry, reread page 19. Then ask two volunteers to act out the scene using a classroom sand box and dump truck. Also draw on real classroom experiences to support comprehension.

On Saturday when I got up
my mother said it was a sunny day
so we could go to the playground
by the pond that has the ducks.

I went there once before
and played on this rope-climbing thing
that looked like a pirate ship.

I was…

23

Excited

24

Social Studies

Discuss with children other things people can share. If not mentioned, name things such as a story, a song, or a special place. Then, invite children to talk about times they have shared things and how it made them feel.

 MEETING INDIVIDUAL NEEDS

Extra Support

Children may be unfamiliar with what a pirate ship looks like. If possible, display some pictures of a pirate ship to help them understand what the piece of playground equipment might have looked like.

2

Interact *with* Literature

READ ALOUD

On Sunday when I called my friend Peter
to see if he could come over to my house to play
his mother said he was sick.

My friend Kate couldn't play either
because she had to do errands with her big brother.

I was...

27

Reading Strategies

▶ **Evaluate**

Reread page 31 for children and evaluate the text for children:

Think Aloud

I think the boy said it had been quite a week because so much had happened during the week to make him feel so many different ways. And I think his father said that he thought most weeks are like that because he knows a lot can happen in week to make a person's feelings change from day to day.

Lonely

28

Self-Assessment

Encourage children to think about their reading by asking themselves these questions:

● Was any part of the story confusing? If so, what part?

● What might I do to help myself understand any confusing part?

Quick**REFERENCE**

Social Studies Link

Recall with children that Katie can't play because she has to do errands with her big brother. Invite children to discuss the different ways they help out at home.

Journal

Help children create a week time-line in their journals. Each day ask children how they feel and help them record their responses. At the end of the week, review all the different emotions that they have felt over the course of the week.

That night when my dad put me to bed
we started talking like we usually do.

I told my dad I thought
it had been quite a week
but my dad said he thought
most weeks are like that.

H-m-m-m...

31

I wonder.

32

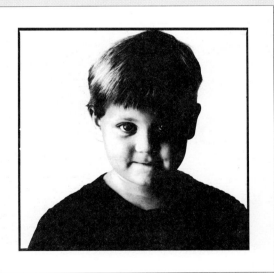

Students Acquiring English

Names for Days of the Week

Review the names of the week with all children. Then pair children acquiring English with fluent English speakers. Then have children work together to point to a week timeline and name the days.

Home Connection

Suggest that children tell this story to family members.

Read Aloud pp. 30–33

MINILESSON

Phonemic Awareness
Rhyming Words

Teach/Model

TESTED SKILL

Ask children to listen while you say two words from the story which have the same last sound: *Dad, had.* Have children say the words with you as they listen for the last sounds. Explain that when two words have the same last sounds we say that the words rhyme. Read the following word pairs for children, and discuss whether or not the words rhyme.

ride	hide

sun	sit

horn	horse

boy	toy

Practice/Apply

Ask children to say "yes" if the words rhyme, and "no" if they don't, as you read the following word pairs:

light	band

jump	neat

fun	run

pig	big

see	bee

long	like

Note any children who seem to have difficulty recognizing words that rhyme. Plan to read more word pairs with them, helping them to tell the difference between words that rhyme and words that do not.

SKILL FINDER Learning About Rhyme, p. T29

Interact with Literature

Rereading

More Choices for Rereading

Likes and Dislikes

Ask children to recall what the boy in the story likes and what he doesn't like. List their responses on chart paper. Suggest that children listen carefully to find out more about what the boy likes and dislikes as you reread the story. Pause to add new entries to the list.

Likes	Doesn't Like
riding his bike	big green monsters
playing with friends	playing alone
drawing pictures	

Act It Out

Students Acquiring English Invite volunteers to act out different scenes as you reread the story page by page. For example, after you read page 11, invite one child to play the teacher and another the boy. Have them act out the teacher looking at the boy's drawing of an elephant.

Timeline

Create a week timeline on the floor. Then have a volunteer stand on the correct space on the timeline as you reread the story.

Informal Assessment

Use the Story Talk or the Retelling activity to assess children's general understanding of the selection.

Responding

Choices for Responding

Retelling *On Monday When It Rained*

Invite pairs of children to take turns retelling the story. Ask one child to turn the pages of the story as the other child looks at the illustrations and tells how the boy feels and why he feels that way.

Students Acquiring English You might pair up children who are acquiring English with native speakers.

A Lot to Be Proud Of

Explain that when we feel proud, it means we feel happy that we can do something well. The boy in the story feels proud of his elephant drawing. Begin a discussion of other things that can make children feel proud, such as learning to do something new or being a helper at home. Invite children to draw a picture and dictate a sentence of something they are proud they can do.

Story Talk

Group children in twos or threes, and have them respond to one or more of the following:

• Tell about times when you have felt disappointed, proud, scared, angry, excited, lonely. How did you show your feelings? Did your face show how you felt?

• Why do you think the boy's father said that most weeks were like the week the boy just had? How often do your feelings change during a week or even during a day?

Portfolio Opportunity

For a writing sample, save children's drawings from A Lot to Be Proud Of.

3

Instruct *and* Integrate

Comprehension

Literacy Activity Book, p. 2

Practice Activities

Noting Details

Extra Support Discuss what children remember about the boy's different feelings and how his face showed how he feels. Take a "picture walk" through the story. As you display each photo, read aloud the feeling word on the left page and ask children to describe any facial details or gestures which help us know that the boy feels that way. Guide children to see that the words and pictures work together to help them understand how the boy is feeling.

More Noting Details

LAB, p. 2

Have children complete *Literacy Activity Book,* page 2, for practice with noting details.

Challenge Invite children to make up stories about one of the other animals on the page. Encourage them to write or dictate their stories, including one or more details about the animal, and create an illustration to go with it.

Faces and Feelings!

Invite children to look through old magazines to cut out pictures showing facial expressions that convey feelings. Encourage them to paste the pictures on construction paper . Ask volunteers to share their work describing how the pictures help us understand how the people are feeling.

Informal Assessment

As children complete the activities, note whether they are able to identify important details. Also observe children's skill in identifying rhyming words.

Phonemic Awareness

Practice Activities

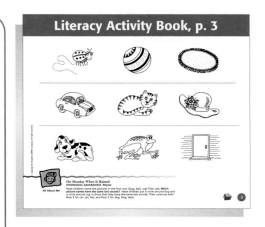

Learning About Rhyme

LAB, p. 3

Extra Support Explain to children that words having the same last sounds are called rhyming words. Say for children several examples of rhyming word pairs such as *cat/hat, dig/ pig,* and *hug/bug.* You may want to ask children to suggest additional words that rhyme with each pair. If necessary, say a few words aloud, for example, *mat* and *fat* and then have children contribute others. Next, invite children to listen as you read aloud the Theme Song *I Am Special, I Am Me* on Teacher's Handbook, page H12. Emphasize the rhyming pairs *me* and *see.* Invite children to suggest other words that rhyme with the word pair.

Have children complete *Literacy Activity Book,* page 3.

Glad or Sad Game

Ask children to think of another feeling word that rhymes with *glad* and *sad.* (mad) Now, invite them to play the "Glad or Sad" Game.

- Tell children that if you say two words that rhyme, like *glad* and *sad,* they should make a glad face.

- Tell them that if you say two words that do not rhyme, like *glad* and *angry,* they should make a sad face.

- Call out rhyming and non-rhyming word pairs, pausing to allow children to respond.

Rain, Rain Go Away!

Recall with children how the boy in the story is disappointed that it rains on Monday because it means he can't play outside. What rhyme might he have said on that day? Invite them to listen as you say the nursery rhyme, "Rain, Rain Go Away."

Say the rhyme again and ask a volunteer to name the two words that rhyme. (away, day) Invite children to think of other words that rhyme with *away* and *day.* (play, pay, stay, may, bay, hay, way)

Challenge Invite children to create a new line or lines for the rhyme.

Rain, rain go away,
Come again another day!

Portfolio Opportunity

Save *Literacy Activity Book,* page 3, as a record of children's understanding of rhyming words.

**Instruct
and
Integrate**

Oral Language

Choices for Oral Language

Story Week

Invite children to make up a class story like *On Monday When It Rained.*

- Ask a volunteer to begin the story by saying, "On Monday_____," and then make up a story event to complete the sentence.

- Then, a second child continues the story by saying, "I felt_____," and telling a feeling to match the event.

- A third and fourth child repeat the procedure for Tuesday.

- Have children continue until they have named all the days of the week. Then begin with Monday again until all children who wish to have had a turn.

My Own Feelings

Discuss with children some events or experiences they have had since school began, that made them feel one of the ways that the boy in the story feels. If necessary, help them get started by asking questions such as:

- When you got on the big school bus for the first time, how did you feel?

- When you painted your first picture, how did you feel?

Feelings Ball

In morning circle, toss a ball to a child who will complete the beginning of a "feeling thought" such as, "I feel happy when…" or "I feel sad when…" Validate each child's feelings and ask classmates for suggestions as to what one might do to ease the pain of sad or uncomfortable feelings or situations.

Materials
- soft-textured ball
- chart paper

Informal Assessment

As children participate in the oral language and writing activities, make note of their ability to listen to others, use temporary and conventional spelling, and convey meaning through their drawings.

 # Writing

Choices for Writing

Weather Words

Remind children that the boy could not ride his bike on Monday because it was rainy. Ask them to name some other weather words. Record them in a word web on chart paper. Then invite children to share experiences they have had in different weather. Have them draw pictures about their experiences and dictate sentences for you to write at the bottom of their pictures. Encourage them to use weather words from the web .

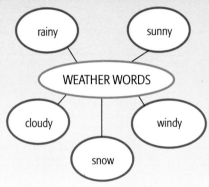

My Friends

Remind children that the boy in the story talked about his friends Maggie, Peter, and Kate. Ask them to name some of their special friends and tell what they like to do together. Then have children draw a picture of a friend in their All About Me Book. (See the Ongoing Project on page T12.) Ask them what they would like you to write on their pictures to tell about their friends.

New Toys for the Sandbox

Remind children that the boy's cousin, Janie, wouldn't let him play with her new dump truck in the sandbox. Draw a sandbox on a large piece of paper, and display it on the wall. Above it, post a sign saying: *Make a new toy for the sandbox.* Read the sign and explain that they can make any kind of toy they wish. Help children label finished toys and tape them to the sandbox.

 **Portfolio Opportunity**

Save children's responses to the Language/Writing Center activities as writing samples.

Instruct *and* Integrate

Cross-Curricular Activities

Choices for Math

Is Peter There, Please?

Extra Support Recall with children how the boy in the story calls his friend Peter to see if he can come over. Write some phone numbers on cards. Pretend to call someone on the phone by displaying the card, and saying the numeral names as you push the buttons. Place the telephones and cards in the Math Center, and encourage children to use the phone numbers when they play telephone.

Materials
- two real (or toy) telephones
- index card for each child

School Days

Display the School Days poster. Discuss with children what happens in the course of a week in the girl's class. Then invite children to draw their own 5-day school calendars and note the special things that happen in your class during the next week.

Students Acquiring English Invite children who are learning English to work with family members to first write the days of the school week on their calendars in their primary language and then write them in English at school.

And Sunday Makes Seven

Remind children that the boy in the story has different feelings on each day of the week. Show children the days of the week on the calendar. Invite children to name the days with you. Then count the days with children explaining that once across the calendar is seven days or one week. Let individuals use a pointer with your help to show other things they already know about a calendar. Have a volunteer lead the others in saying the names of the days of the week again.

Materials
- a calendar for a month
- pointer

Poster

Music

Mood Music

Remind children that in the story the boy feels many different ways. Tell them that often music can make people feel different ways. Invite children to listen to different music and ask how it makes them feel. Encourage them to explain why it makes them feel that way.

Challenge Encourage children to use simple instruments to create their own "mood music." Ask the class to guess what feeling the music expresses. Invite them to tell what feeling slow or fast, loud or soft music creates.

Materials
- a variety of tapes or records of different background music
- hand-held musical instruments

Art

Colors and Feelings

Discuss with children how different colors are sometimes associated with certain feelings—red with anger, blue with sadness, yellow with fear. Then have them choose one feeling mentioned in the story and a color of paint that they think shows that feeling. Ask them to paint a picture of the boy's face in that color. Encourage them to share their paintings with the class and explain why they chose the color they did.

Materials
- paints
- paper

BIG BOOK
SELECTION:
ABC and You

Big Book

Little Big Book

by Eugenie Fernandes

**Other Books by
Eugenie Fernandes**
One Light, One Sun

Selection Summary

ABC and You is a unique alphabet book. Each letter is represented by a pair of words: an adjective and a child's name that begins with that letter. Children will have a marvelous time learning the alphabet as they meet children like themselves.

Lesson Planning Guide

	Skill/Strategy Instruction	Meeting Individual Needs	Lesson Resources
1 **Introduce** *the* **Literature** *Pacing: 1 day*	**Shared Reading and Writing** Warm-Up/Build Background, T36 Shared Reading, T36 Shared Writing, T37	**Choices for Rereading**, T37	**Poster** ABC Song *Literacy Activity Book* Personal Response, p. 4
2 **Interact** *with* **Literature** *Pacing: 1-2 days*	**Reading Strategies** Predict/Infer, T38 Monitor, T38, T46 Think About Words, T42 Evaluate, T44, T48 **Minilessons** ✔ Letter as Letter, T39 ✔ Sequence, T43 Noting Details, T45 ✔ Letter Names, T49	**Students Acquiring English,** T44, T48, T50 **Extra Support,** T38, T40, T46 **Challenge,** T42, T51 **Rereading and Responding,** T50–T51	*Literacy Activity Book* Language Patterns, p. 5 **Story Props,** T51 **Audio Tape** for All About Me: *ABC and You* See the Houghton Mifflin **Internet** resources for additional activities.
3 **Instruct** *and* **Integrate** *Pacing: 1-2 days*	**Reading/Listening Center** Comprehension, T52 Concept Development, T53 Concepts About Print, T54 Listening, T55 **Language/Writing Center** Oral Language, T56 Writing, T57 **Cross-Curricular Center** Cross-Curricular Activities, T58–T59	**Extra Support,** T52, T53, T54, T57 **Students Acquiring English,** T55, T56 **Challenge,** T52, T59	*My Big Dictionary,* T53, T54, T57 **Game:** Alphabet Adventure, T53, H6 *Literacy Activity Book* Comprehension, p. 7 Concept Development, p. 8 **Audio Tape** for All About Me: *ABC and You* See the Houghton Mifflin **Internet** resources for additional activities.

✔ *Indicates Tested Skills. See page T11 for assessment options.*

1 Introduce *the* Literature

Shared Reading and Writing

Poster

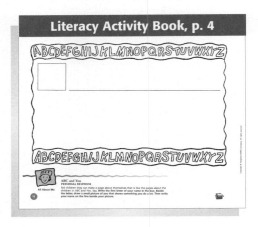

ABC Song

A, B, C, D, E, F, G,
H, I, J, K, L-M-N-O-P,
Q, R, S and T, U, V,
W, X, and Y, and Z.

Now I know my ABC's,
Next time won't you sing with me?

Literacy Activity Book, p. 4

ABCDEFGHIJKLMNOPQRSTUVWXYZ

ABCDEFGHIJKLMNOPQRSTUVWXYZ

INTERACTIVE LEARNING

Warm-Up/Build Background

Sharing a Song
- Display the poster for "ABC Song" and direct children's attention to the letters printed on it. Ask children what these are called. (letters of the alphabet)

- Invite children to follow along as you read or sing "ABC Song," pointing to the different letters.

- Have volunteers point to the letters as you sing the song with children as many times as they want to.

- Encourage children to share other ABC songs or rhymes they know and to talk about what they know about the alphabet.

Shared Reading

LAB, p. 4

Preview and Predict

Display *ABC and You* and point to and read the title. Tell children that this book tells about children with names that begin with all the different letters of the alphabet. Explain that in an alphabet book like this one, they can expect to see the letters come in the same order as they do when they sing the ABC song. Ask children what letter of the alphabet they should see first. *(A)* Then display the first few pages, allowing children to name the letters and discuss the illustrations.

Read Together

Read the book for children, including the letter name *("A... Amazing Amanda")* to emphasize the letters of the alphabet. Pause for children who wish to comment about names that are the same as their own, names of people they know, or the letters that their own names begin with.

Personal Response

Ask children to tell what they liked best about the alphabet book. Then have them complete *Literacy Activity Book,* page 4.

Shared Writing: *A Class Story*

Prewriting

Remind children that the story *ABC and You* introduces children whose names began with all the different letters of the alphabet. Invite them to help you write a class story with their names in it. At the top of a chart paper write *ABC and Us.* Say the title as you write it. Then ask them to think about what letter their first name begins with. As you say the alphabet slowly, help children to get in a line according to the letter their first name begins with.

Drafting

- Write and say the following: We are in (your name)'s kindergarten class. Our names begin with letters of the alphabet. Let us introduce ourselves.

- Starting with the first child in line, have each child fill in the blanks with your help as you write:

  (the letter child's first name begins with) **My name is** (child's name.)

- Model for children the correct formation of each capital letter.

ABC and Us

We are in Mr. Kim's class. Our names begin with letters of the alphabet. Let us introduce ourselves.

    A   My name is Alice.

    B   My name is Billy.

    B   My name is Bob.

    D   My name is Dawn.

    J   My name is Juanita.

Publishing

Rewrite the story into book form with a page for each child. If possible, put children's photos on the pages with their names so they can read the book independently.

Choices for Rereading

Rereadings provide varied, repeated experiences with the literature so that children can make its language and content their own. The following rereading choices appear on page T50.

- Listen and Read!
- Recognizing Language Patterns
- Noting Text and Picture Details
- Concepts About Print

Portfolio Opportunity

Save *Literacy Activity Book,* page 4, for a record of children's reponses to the selection.

Interact with Literature

Reading Strategies

▶ **Predict/Infer Monitor**

Discussion Ask children how thinking about the order of the alphabet and the story pattern (an alphabet letter then a describing word and name) can help them figure out what comes next in the story.

Purpose Setting

As your reread the story with children, suggest that they ask for help during reading if they hear a word they don't understand. Encourage them to use picture-clues to figure it out.

BIG BOOK

A Amazing Amanda

B Brave Ben

QuickREFERENCE

Journal

Ask children to keep track of the letters that appear in the story by printing them in their journals.

Extra Support

Word Meaning Have children describe what each child is doing. Then use their responses to define unfamiliar words. For example, Brave Ben is protecting the kitten from the dog. You might say: *If a person is brave like Ben, they are not afraid to protect a kitten from a dog. A brave person is not afraid.*

5

 Curious Caroline

7

MINILESSON

Concepts of Print

Letter as Letter

Teach/Model

TESTED SKILL

Display page 4 and point to the letter *A*. Tell children that this is a letter and that words are made up of letters, and that knowing letters will help them read words. Then, write the following on the board:

* 3 A

Invite a volunteer to point to the letter.

Practice/Apply

Display other letters in the story, write them on the board with other types of symbols and ask children to distinguish between the letters and non-letters.

SKILL FINDER What's a Letter? page T54

Math Link/Visual Literacy

Invite volunteers to count how many fish or shells appear on pages 4 and 5.

Science Link

Explain that while people breathe oxygen from the air, almost all fish breathe oxygen from the water. They do this by swallowing water through their mouth and pumping it over their gills. Fish can't survive for long out of the water, just as people can't be underwater for a long period of time unless they have special equipment.

BIG BOOK

D Daring Dan

F Freckled Freddie

Background: FYI

The classical ballet technique began in France in the 1600's. Even today, the names of all the steps and positions in ballet are French words.

Extra Support

MEETING INDIVIDUAL NEEDS

Word Meaning For unfamiliar words such as *daring, energetic,* and *graceful,* note details in the pictures which support the definitions.

Concept Review

Feelings Recall how our faces often show how we feel. Then invite children to tell you why *Happy Henry* is a good name for the child in the picture on page 11. How does his face show he is happy? *(smiling)*

Energetic Emily

9

Graceful Gloria

Happy Henry

11

Interact *with* Literature

BIG BOOK

I Ill Ida

12

Reading Strategies

► **Thinking About Words**

Ask children how they could figure out the meaning of *ill* on page 12 if they did not know the word.

What makes sense I know from the pattern of the story that this word tells about the child, Ida.

Picture Clues I see Ida in bed with a thermometer in her mouth. When I am sick, my mom takes my temperature. I think *ill* must mean *sick*.

K Kind Kim

QuickREFERENCE

Math Link/Visual Literacy

Talk about why the name *Little Lucy* makes sense. Encourage children to compare the size of the girl in relationship to the dog in the picture. Explain to children that Lucy will grow taller as she gets older.

Challenge

Social Studies/Visual Literacy
Challenge children to tell you where they think the girl and kittens are in the picture on page 14. *(a barn)*

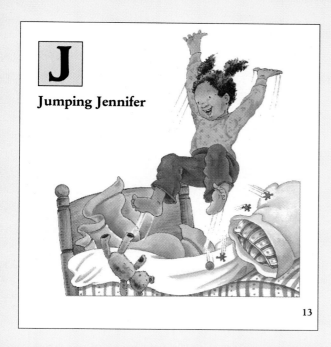

J Jumping Jennifer

13

L Little Lucy

15

Comprehension

Sequence

TESTED SKILL

Teach/Model

Display an alphabet strip of capital letters and invite children to read the letter names with you. Explain to them that whenever letters are in this special order, they are called the alphabet. Ask children to name the first letter of the alphabet. Then ask them to name the last letter. Then point to a letter in the middle of the alphabet and ask them to name the letter and to tell which letter comes next.

Tell children that an alphabet story, such as this one, should follow the special order of the alphabet. Knowing this, ask them to tell you what letter should appear first in the story (A), what letter should come next (B), and so on. Turn the pages with children to check whether the story follows this sequence.

Practice/Apply

Have children look at page 15 and name the letter. Then ask them to predict what letter will appear on the next page. Turn the page to check their predictions. Repeat this procedure with other right-hand pages.

SKILL FINDER

ABC and You Sequence, page T52

Minilessons, See Themes 3, 8

Interact *with* Literature

Reading Strategies

▶ **Evaluate**

After reading through page 19, pause to ask children how they feel about the story so far. Use the following prompts as needed:

- Do you like the story so far? Why or why not?

- Which name do you like the most? Why?

- Which character do you think you are the most like? Why?

M Marvelous Matthew

16

O Organized Olivia

P Proud Peter

18

QuickREFERENCE

Math Link

Display page 17 and ask children when most people take naps—at night or during the day.

Students Acquiring English

Word Meaning Explain to the class that *organized* means neat and orderly as you point out the lined up stuffed animals on page 18. If children acquiring English still seem confused, point out an area of the classroom that is messy, and invite a volunteer to make it neat. When the child is finished, say: This area was messy, now it is organized.

 Napping Noah

17

Q Quiet Quincy

19

Comprehension

Review: Noting Details

Teach/Model

Model for children how to use picture clues to figure out why Peter feels *proud*.

Think Aloud

I see that Peter is riding a horse and by the smile on his face I can tell he is happy. The ribbon on the horse has a number one on it. That is a first prize ribbon. I think Peter and his horse won first prize for something. If I won first prize I would feel proud too.

Practice/Apply

Ask children to tell what happened when Quincy sat quietly outdoors. Encourage them to note picture clues. *(Birds and animals came to him. A butterfly landed on his hand.)*

Science Link

Name the different animals on page 19 with children. *(Quails, butterfly, rabbit, chipmunk, bird, squirrel)* Then ask: Would the animals be coming up so close to Quincy if he was being noisy? Why or why not?

Interact *with* Literature

R Royal Rosie

20

Reading Strategies

▶ **Monitor**

After children have read page 23 with you, ask if it makes sense that the character is called *Unhappy Ursula.* Encourage them to note the picture details such as the rain and the picnic basket and to draw some conclusions about why she might be unhappy. For example, they might conclude that the little girl was planning to go on a picnic, but because of the rain she can't go.

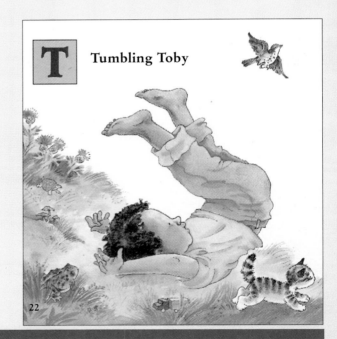

T Tumbling Toby

22

QuickREFERENCE

Science Link

Invite children to blow their own bubbles by using bubble liquid. Talk about what happens when the outside of a bubble is broken. (the bubble disappears) Ask children what they think was inside the bubble. (air)

Extra Support

Word Meaning Encourage children to tell you who the girl is pretending to be on page 20. (a *queen* or a *king*) Explain that *royal* means something to do with a king or queen. You might want to display some pictures of kings and queens to help them understand how Rosie's clothing makes her royal.

Soapy Sylvie

21

 Unhappy Ursula

23

Big Book pp. 21, 23

Movement Link

Have children practice tumbling on mats. Explain that tumbling is a form of gymnastics or acrobatics.

Concept Review

Feelings Ask children how we can tell by looking at the girl's face on page 23 that she is unhappy. (her frown) Challenge them to remember other feeling words that mean unhappy. (disappointed, sad) Then have them recall why the boy in *On Monday When It Rained* was unhappy or disappointed. (He couldn't ride his bike to his friend's house in the rain.)

Interact with Literature

BIG BOOK

Reading Strategies

▶ **Evaluate**

Tell children that good readers tell whether or not they liked the story. Then, invite them to take turns telling how they felt about the story.

V Victorious Vickie

W Wet Walter

Y Yawning Yolanda

Z Zippity Zack

26

Self-Assessment

Invite children to talk about the predictions they made as they read the story.

- Were they able to make better predictions as they got to know the story pattern?
- How did knowing the alphabet help?
- What else did they do to make sure they understood the story?

Quick**REFERENCE**

Journal

After completing the story, invite volunteers to name all the letters they printed in their journals.

Students Acquiring English

Word Meaning Explain to children that the girl on page 24 has won the race, so she is *victorious*. If children acquiring English still seem confused, stage a running race outside with a finish line. Tell them that the child who crosses the finish line first will be victorious.

Excited Xavier

25

... and You!

MINILESSON

Concept Development

Letter Names

Teach/Model

Explain to children that words are made up of letters, and that each letter has a name, just like they each have a name. Page through the Big Book, pointing to the letters as you say their names. Repeat the procedure having children join you in naming the letters.

Practice/Apply

Display random pages from the story, and invite volunteers to name the letters.

SKILL FINDER Naming the Capital Letters, page T53

Visual Literacy

Invite children to tell you why they think Xavier is excited or happy. Encourage them to note picture details to help them draw their own conclusions.

Social Studies Link

Explain to children that traveling can be exciting because it is an opportunity to see different places and meet different people. Collect some travel brochures and allow children to look through them. Invite them to choose a place to visit.

2

Interact with Literature

Rereading

Literacy Activity Book, p. 5

Choices for Rereading

Listen and Read!

Audio Tape for All About Me: *ABC and You*

Place the Audio Tape and copies of the Little Big Book *ABC and You* in the Reading/Listening Center. Invite children to follow along in the books as they listen to the tape.

Noting Text and Picture Details

Tell children that during this reading of the story, you will stop to talk with them about what is in the pictures. Read page 4 with children and then ask them to name some things they see in the picture. List the things children name on the board, and then invite volunteers to underline the words that begin with *a*. Follow a similar procedure with each page.

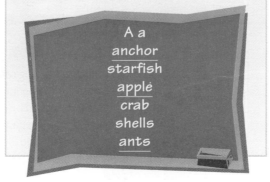

Recognizing Language Patterns
LAB, p. 5

As children read the story with you, help them note the repeating language pattern by pointing out the letter, the describing word, and the child's name on each page.

Provide practice with story language patterns by having children complete *Literacy Activity Book,* page 5.

Students Acquiring English Help children to act out each word on the activity page and then to use the word to complete a simple sentence: "I am _____."

Concepts About Print

To help children match spoken letter names to printed letters, invite volunteers to take turns framing the individual letters as you read with the group.

Informal Assessment

Use the Personal Response and the other responding activities to assess children's general understanding of the selection. Also note children's ability to match spoken and written letters.

Responding to the Story

Choices for Responding

Alphabet Soup

- Distribute the precut alphabet letters to small groups of children to decorate, using words and pictures taken from the page of the story where the letter appears.

- Then put the decorated letters in a bowl or pot, stir them around, and spoon a letter out to each group.

- Children in each group take turns describing, but not showing, the letter to the class. Then the class tries to guess the letter.

Materials
- precut oak tag alphabet letters

Using Story Props

Invite volunteers to choose a stick-on letter and say its name and then a describing word and person's name to go with the letter.

Materials
- Story Retelling Props (See Teacher's Handbook, page H2.)

Personal Response

Invite children to talk about the different characters in the selection. What did they learn about each one? Which one did they like the most? Why? Ask children to draw a picture of the character they liked most. Help them copy the letter and the character's name onto their picture. Suggest that they share their pictures with their families and use the text to recall the story's language pattern.

Nicknames

Invite children to recall some of the describing words that were part of the children's names in the story. Then ask the children to think about a word that best describes themselves. Write each child's choice before their name and read aloud their new nickname. Encourage children to write their new nicknames in their All About Me Books. (See the Ongoing Project, page T12.)

Challenge Some children may want to try to find an appropriate describing word that begins with the same letter as their name.

Comprehension

Literacy Activity Book, p. 7

Practice Activities

ABC and You Sequence

Extra Support Have the class say the alphabet as you write the letters on the board. Remind them that in an alphabet book like *ABC and You,* they can expect the letters to appear in this same order.

- Invite a volunteer to open up the Big Book to any two pages. Read the pages aloud, including the letters.

- Challenge the child to find the same two letters that are on the pages on the board and circle them.

- Ask the class: Which letter comes first? next? What letter do you think will come next if we continue reading? If children are unsure of the letter names, have them point to the letters on the board.

- Then turn the page to check their predictions.

- Repeat this activity with different volunteers.

Sequence Practice

LAB, p.7

Have children complete *Literacy Activity Book,* page 7, for more practice with alphabetical order or sequence.

Sequencing Names

Write the letters of the alphabet on index cards. Place the cards alphabetically on the floor. Then, ask children to stand next to the letter on the floor that their name begins with. If children's names begin with the same letter, have them stand side by side. If necessary, explain that some of the letters have no one standing by them because there aren't any names in the class which begin with those letters.

Challenge Invite volunteers to tally results to see which letter is at the beginning of the most class names.

Informal Assessment

As children complete the activities, note how well they understand alphabetical order.

Concept Development

Practice Activities

Naming the Capital Letters

LAB, p.8

Extra Support Remind children that words are made of letters, and that knowing the letters will help them to read words. Display *My Big Dictionary*, read the title, and explain that this book has all of the alphabet letters. As you display each page, have a volunteer name the capital letter.

Home Connection Have children take home completed *Literacy Activity Book* page 8 and practice naming the letters with a family member.

Capital and Small Letter Names

Explain to children that each letter name has two letters— a capital and a small letter.

- Turn to page 2 of *My Big Dictionary* and invite a volunteer to identify capital *A* and small *a*.

- Help children identify each picture. Point out that the word that accompanies each picture begins with small *a*.

- Follow this procedure as you move through the alphabet pages one letter at a time.

More with Letter Names

Invite children to look at the alphabet scene on page 3 in *My Big Dictionary*. Ask them to name things they see in the picture. List the things children name on the board, and then invite volunteers to underline the words that begin with *a*. Follow this procedure as you move through the alphabet scenes one letter at a time. Then point to the first letter of each word on your list and have children name the letters with you.

Alphabet Adventure

Let children play the game with partners or in small groups to practice naming capital letters.

Materials
- Game: Alphabet Adventure (See Teacher's Handbook, page H6.)

Literacy Activity Book, p. 8

My Big Dictionary

Portfolio Opportunity

Save *Literacy Activity Book* page 7 as a record of children's understanding of alphabetical order.

Instruct *and* **Integrate**

Concepts About Print

Practice Activities

My Big Dictionary

What's a Letter?

Extra Support Display an alphabet page in *My Big Dictionary.* Point to the capital and small letter and remind children that these are letters, that words are made up of letters, and that knowing letters will help them read words. Then invite children to come up to an alphabet page and point to and count the letters in the words.

Capital or Small

Display *My Big Dictionary* and remind children that each letter name has a capital and a small letter.

- Invite volunteers to identify the capital and small letter on each alphabet page and then name the letter.

- Now display page 4 in *ABC and You* and frame the word *Amazing* as you read it. Explain to children that this word is made up of letters.

- Invite a volunteer to come up to the Big Book and, with your help, point to each letter in the word. Ask another volunteer to find the capital letter in the word and point to it. Follow this procedure with other words from the story.

Names in Print

Display page 4 of *ABC and You* and frame the name *Amanda.* Explain to children that names begin with a capital letter followed by small letters. Read the name and identify the capital and small letters for children. Distribute name cards and help children identify the capital letter in their name and then the small letters.

Informal Assessment

As children engage in the activities, note their ability to point out and listen for letters.

Listening

Practice Activities

Listen and Read!

Audio Tape for All About Me: *ABC and You*

Place copies of the Little Big Book *ABC and You* along with the Audio Tape in the Reading/Listening Center. Have children match the spoken letters to print by pointing to each letter as the narrator reads.

Find the Letter

- Distribute markers and an alphabet strip to pairs of children.

- Explain to children that you are going to name a letter and they are to work together to find the letter on the alphabet strip and put a marker on it.

Students Acquiring English Have children who are acquiring English work with native speakers on this activity.

Materials
- alphabet strips made from adding machine tape
- small objects to use as markers

Who Am I Describing?

Remind children that the story *ABC and You* describes different characters. Explain to children that you are going to describe someone in the class and their job is to listen carefully for details that will help them name the child being described. Repeat the activity so several children are described.

Instruct
and
Integrate

Oral Language

Choices for Oral Language

Talking About Words

Discuss the describing words in *ABC and You* with children.

For example, use questions such as the following to begin a discussion of *kind:* Does a kind person share? Does a kind person say mean things to someone? Does a kind person take turns?

Then have children suggest things that a kind kindergartner would do. Follow a similar procedure with other describing words.

Sharing Experiences

Help children complete the following sentence starter:

I was brave when I_____.

Repeat the procedure by replacing *brave* with *curious, kind, daring, energetic, graceful, happy, proud, unhappy, excited.*

Students Acquiring English Pair up fluent English speakers with children acquiring English. Have them work together to act out situations that illustrate the meaning of each word on the list and say the completed sentence starter together.

Where Have We Seen Letters?

Have children talk about all the different places they see or have seen letters. You might start a class list of the many places letters appear and invite children to make suggestions to add to it throughout the theme.

Informal Assessment

As children complete the activities, note their interest in and ability with theme-related, listening-speaking vocabulary. Also observe their ability to print the letters of the alphabet.

 # Writing

Choices for Writing

Writing the Alphabet Letters

Tell children that naming and printing the letters of the alphabet will help them read and write words that contain these letters.

- Display page 2 of *My Big Dictionary*.

- Trace the letters with a finger as children say the letter name aloud.

- Have children trace the letters on their desktops, or the palm of their hand, as you name the letter.

- Then, invite them to practice printing each of the letters on sheets of paper.

- Repeat the procedure for the remaining alphabet pages in *My Big Dictionary*.

My Big Dictionary

Feeling the ABC's

 Extra Support Use white glue to form the alphabet letters on a strip of paper. Leave it in a "ridge" as it comes out of the bottle and let it dry. Children can trace over the letters with their fingers.

Sentence Strips

On a large sentence strip, write:

> **I like to** _____ .

Display pictures of children doing things such as swinging, swimming, and dancing. Talk with children about the pictures. Have them choose one of the pictured activities and complete the sentence strip with the word that describes what the child in the picture is doing. Then give each child a blank sentence strip and explain that they can copy your sentence strip and finish it with a word that tells what *they* like to do. Children may want to add their sentence strips to their All About Me book. (See the Ongoing Project, page T12.)

Portfolio Opportunity

Invite children to save copies of their printed letters and their sentence strips.

Instruct
and
Integrate

Cross-Curricular Activities

Choices for Creative Movement

Body Letters

Recall the different letter symbols with children. Then invite pairs to choose a letter and then work together to form it with their bodies. Invite the others to name the letter they have formed.

Name Cheers

Choose a volunteer to lead classmates in a cheer. Give the leader his or her name card. Then distribute letter cards for each letter of that name to other children.

Materials
- name cards

- The leader looks at his or her name card and says: *Give me a* <names the first letter.>

- The child with that letter card jumps up, repeats the letter, and then joins the leader at the front of the room while displaying the letter card to the class.

- Repeat this procedure with the remaining letters of the leader's name.

- When all the letters have been called, the leader shouts out his or her name and the children with the letter cards jump up and shout out the name.

- Repeat the procedure until all interested children have had the opportunity to lead a cheer for their name.

Art

Crayon Rubbings

Invite children to make their names look special.

- Provide children with the letters in their names.

- Ask each child, with your help, to spell out his or her name with the sandpaper letters and to tape them onto a table or desktop.

- Next, have children place a piece of construction paper over the letters in their name and then rub over them using different colors and surfaces of crayons.

Materials
- precut letters from sandpaper or other textured materials
- construction paper
- crayons
- tape

Math

How Many Letters ?

Challenge Provide children with name cards and 10–12 interlocking cubes.

- Ask children to count the number of letters in their name and then count out the same number of cubes.

- Then ask them to check if they counted the correct number of cubes by placing a cube on top of each letter in their name. Invite volunteers to tell you how many letters are in their name and record the numerals next to their names.

- Have a volunteer collect any leftover cubes. Then have pairs switch name cards and place their cubes on top of each letter in the name. Ask: Does your partner have more, fewer, or the same number of letters as your name? How do you know?

Materials
- interlocking cubes
- name cards

BIG BOOK

SELECTION:
Faces

by Shelley Rotner and
Ken Kreisler

**Other Books by Shelley Rotner
and Ken Kreisler**

Nature Spy

Citybook

Ocean Day

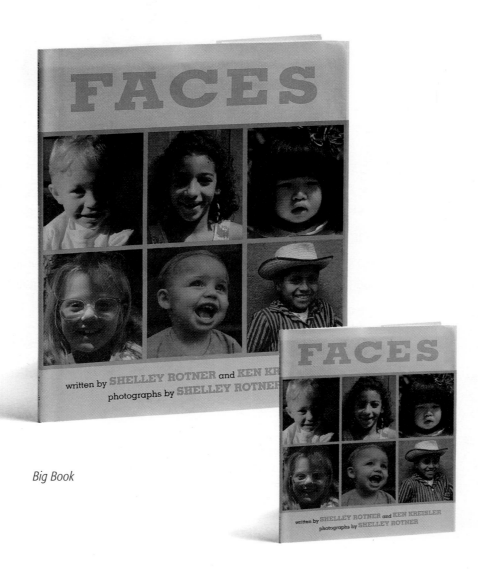

Big Book

Little Big Book

Selection Summary

With colorful photographs of children from all over the world, the text tells
how children's faces are alike because they have the same features and
express the same feelings, but different because each person is an individual.

Lesson Planning Guide

	Skill/Strategy Instruction	Meeting Individual Needs	Lesson Resources
1 Introduce *the* Literature *Pacing: 1 day*	**Shared Reading and Writing** Warm-Up/Build Background, T62 Shared Reading, T62 Shared Writing, T63	**Choices for Rereading,** T63 **Students Acquiring English,** T63	**Poster** Reflection, T62 *Literacy Activity Book* Personal Response, p. 9
2 Interact *with* Literature *Pacing: 1–2 days*	**Reading Strategies** Summarize, T64, T76 Evaluate, T64, T68 Monitor, T72 Predict/Infer, T74 **Minilessons** ✔ Book Handling, T65 ✔ Categorize and Classify, T69 Parts of the Body, T75	**Students Acquiring English,** T74, T75, T80 **Extra Support,** T64, T68 **Challenge,** T65, T67, T76, T77 **Rereading and Responding,** T80–T81	*Literacy Activity Book* Language Patterns, p. 10 **Audio Tape** for All About Me: *Faces* See the Houghton Mifflin **Internet** resources for additional activities.
3 Instruct *and* Integrate *Pacing: 1–2 days*	**Reading/Listening Center** Comprehension, T82 Concept Development, T83 Concepts About Print, T84 Listening, T85 **Independent Reading and Writing** T86–T87 **Language/Writing Center** Oral Language, T88 Writing, T89 **Cross-Curricular Center** Cross-Curricular Activities, T90–T91	**Extra Support,** T82, T83, T84 **Challenge,** T82, T84 **Students Acquiring English,** T85	**Poster** Look at Me!, T90 *Literacy Activity Book* Comprehension, p. 11 Concept Development, p. 12 **Audio Tape** for All About Me: *Faces*

✔ *Indicates Tested Skills. See page T11 for assessment options.*

1

Introduce *the* Literature

Shared Reading and Writing

Poster

Reflection

In the mirror
I can see
Lots of things
But mostly-me.

MYRA COHN LIVINGSTON

Poster: All About Me

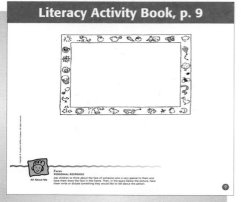

Literacy Activity Book, p. 9

Faces
PERSONAL RESPONSE

All About Me

Warm-Up/Build Background

Sharing Poetry
- Invite children to follow along as you read the poster for "Reflection."
- After reading, provide a handheld mirror for children to look in.
- Encourage them to describe what they see.
- Then read the poem again, pausing to allow children to supply the word *me* at the end.

Shared Reading

LAB, p. 9

Preview and Predict
- Display the cover of *Faces.* Read the title of the book and name the two authors. Explain that Shelley Rotner also took the photographs.
- Remind children that good readers think about what a story might be about before they read it.
- Discuss the photographs on the cover and have children tell you what they think they will read about in this book. Record their suggestions on the board. Then suggest that they read the story with you to find out if their predictions match the story.

Read Together
- Read the story together, encouraging children to join in when they can.
- As you read, pause briefly to allow children to revise any of their predictions and to comment on any photographs that have special meaning to them.

Personal Response
Have children complete *Literacy Activity Book* page 9.

Shared Writing: *Class Story*

Prewriting

Have children put their hands up to their faces and name their features as they touch them. Record their suggestions in a word web.

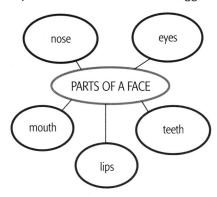

Drafting

- At the top of a piece of chart paper, write *My Face,* reading the words aloud as you write them.

- Then write and say: *I see with my* _____. (eyes) Ask children to supply the word to finish the sentence. If necessary, review the words they generated in the word web.

- Continue by replacing *see* with *hear, smell, talk, chew, smile,* encouraging children to supply ways that they use their faces.

Publishing and Sharing

Read the chart story with children, asking if there is anything they would like to add to it or change. Then display the story on the theme bulletin board. (See Launching the Theme, page T12.) You may also want to have volunteers illustrate the words in the word web and display it in the Writing Center.

Students Acquiring English Shared writing activities allow children acquiring English to contribute according to their proficiency level—by offering suggestions, chiming in, or simply following along.

Choices for Rereading

Rereadings provide varied, repeated experiences with the literature so that children can make its language and content their own. The following rereading choices appear on page T80.

- Noting Language Patterns

- Listen and Read!

- Listen and Point

- Fill in the Blank

Interact
with
Literature

Reading Strategies

▶ **Summarize**
 Evaluate

Student Application Remind children that good readers look for the most important parts of a story so they will understand and remember it. They also think about how they feel about a story. Help children recall how they used these strategies for *On Monday When It Rained* and *ABC and You.*

Predicting/Purpose Setting

Suggest that as children reread the story, they pay attention to the most important parts to help them remember it. You might encourage them to copy the first line of the story *(Faces, faces, all kinds of faces.)* in their journals to help them remember the beginning of the story. Then, have them draw pictures of the faces and events they think are most important to remember as they read.

BIG BOOK

4   Faces, faces, all kinds of faces.

6   Faces talking,

QuickREFERENCE

Science Link

Point out the shadows on page 6. Explain to children that a shadow occurs when something blocks out light from the sun. Invite children to experiment with shadows outside.

Extra Support

If children seem confused by the phrase *all kinds of faces,* point out that there are many different faces pictured—none are exactly alike. There are baby faces, smiling faces, and so on.

5

faces smelling,

7

Concepts About Print

Book Handling

Teach/Model

TESTED ✓ SKILL

- Display the Big Book *Faces.* Model for children how to hold a book right side up, and turn the pages.

- Then invite a different volunteer to show you where the book begins and where it ends. If necessary, show children that the front cover is the beginning of the book and the back cover is the end.

- Open the book to page 4. Suggest that each page of the book also has a beginning and an end. Explain that as we read the words on each page, we go from the first word to the last word. Point out where you will begin reading on this page. Then, read the page aloud sweeping your hand under the words from left to right.

Practice/Apply

Provide copies of the Little Big Book to children. Have them show how to read each page by placing a finger under the first word on a page and then moving it under the words left to right until they reach the last word.

SKILL FINDER → Right Side Up, T84

Science Link

Ask children what part of their face they use to smell. Point out that the flower on page 7 smells good. Discuss some other things that smell good.

MEETING INDIVIDUAL NEEDS

Challenge

Concepts About Print Point to the commas and explain to children that when they see that mark, which is called a comma, it means to take a little breath and then continue to read to the end of the sentence.

Interact
with
Literature

BIG BOOK

faces hearing,

8

Thinking faces,

10

QuickREFERENCE

Science Link

Point out that the girl is whispering (speaking quietly) in the other girl's ear. Invite children to discuss different loud and soft sounds.

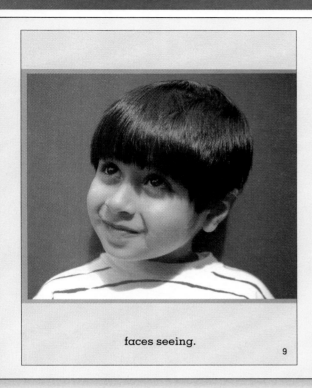

faces seeing.

9

sleeping faces,

11

Social Studies Link

Ask children if they know people who do not see well or hear well. Explain that blind people can read with their fingers and that deaf people can listen with their eyes and talk with their hands.

MEETING INDIVIDUAL NEEDS

Challenge

Challenge children to use their eyes like the boy on page 9. Display several objects on a table. Give interested children 30 seconds to look at the table. Have each child turn around and try to name what objects are on the table.

Interact *with* **Literature**

BIG BOOK

Reading Strategies

▶ **Evaluate**

Discuss what children think about the story so far.

- Do they like how the authors use photographs to show what faces can do?

- What else do they like or not like about the story?

12   friendly faces,

14   Funny faces

QuickREFERENCE

Math Link

Ask children if the funny faces on page 14 make them laugh. Then, invite them to work with a partner to count how many different funny faces they can make. Encourage them to share their findings.

Extra Support

Word Meaning Explain that dogs are like friends to many people. Ask: Do you think the dog is this boy's friend? How can you tell? Explain that *friendly* means behaving as you would with a friend—being warm and welcoming.

faces feeling.

13

15

Comprehension

Categorize and Classify

TESTED SKILL

Teach/Model

Have children look at the pictures on pages 14–15 and explain why they think the authors put these faces together. Point out that it is often useful to group together things that are alike in some way. Then, invite children to make some faces that would go with the ones pictured.

Practice/Apply

Have children make faces that could go with some of the other face groupings in the story. (thinking faces, sleeping faces, and so on) Then, invite volunteers to suggest other kinds of faces they could make (yawning faces, sad faces, and so on) and have the rest of the class make them.

SKILL FINDER

Categorize and Classify, p. T82

Minilesson, See Theme 5

Concept Review

Remind children that people can often tell how you're feeling by the expression on your face. Challenge them to guess how each child on page 13 is feeling by looking at the expression on their face. (sad, angry, happy, excited/surprised)

BIG BOOK

sometimes masked,

16

sometimes painted.

18

QuickREFERENCE

★★ Multicultural Link

Tell children that people in many places in the world wear masks or paint their faces for special occasions. Invite them to name times that people in the United States use masks.

🏠 Home Connection

Suggest that children tell their families about the masks in *Faces*. Families might like to make masks together at home using paper plates and markers.

17

19

Background: FYI

Clowns paint their faces to help make people laugh. Clowns have been around since ancient times. They used to be called jesters, fools, and buffoons.

Interact
with
Literature

Reading Strategies

▶ **Monitor**

After children have read pages 20–23 with you, ask them to explain in their own words how faces are *All different, each special in its own way.* If they have difficulty, help them review the illustrations on pages 4–23. Encourage children to use what they see in the pictures and what they already knew about faces before reading the story to help in their explanations of how faces are special.

BIG BOOK

All different,

20

each special in its own way.

22

Quick REFERENCE

Social Studies Link

Explain to children that their faces are special or unique. Ask them what would happen if everyone looked the same. (You wouldn't be able to tell people apart; it would be too boring!)

21

23

Math Link

Ask children what their favorite ice cream flavors are. Have them vote for their favorite and tally the results to see which flavor your class likes the most.

Interact
with
Literature

Reading Strategies

▶ **Predict/Infer**

After reading page 25, ask children how they could predict what other parts of the face they will read about. How can knowing what the author said faces can do earlier in this story help?

BIG BOOK

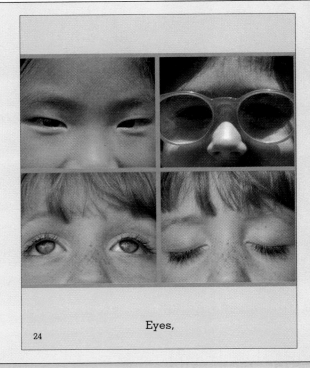

Eyes,

24

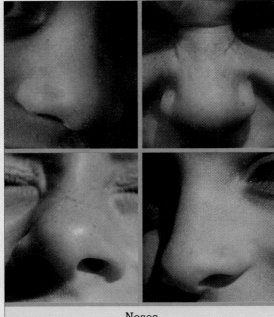

Noses,

26

QuickREFERENCE

Math Link

Draw an eye, ear, nose, and mouth on the board. Ask: How many of each feature do you have? Have a volunteer record the number for an individual next to each image.

Students Acquiring English

Invite volunteers who speak a different language to teach the class their words for different facial features. Then the volunteers can say each word, and have classmates point at the correct feature.

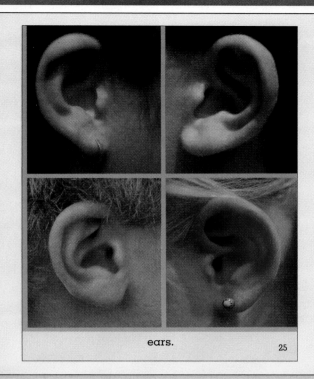

ears.

25

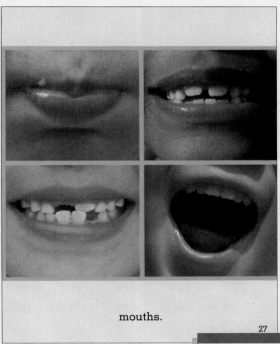

mouths.

27

Big Book pp. 25, 27

Concept Development

Parts of the Body

Teach/Model

Reread pages 24–27 in the Big Book, and explain to children that our faces are part of our bodies and that our eyes, ears, noses, mouths are parts of our bodies too. Then, stand at the front of the room and point to different parts of your body such as an arm, leg, hip, and so on and invite the class to name them.

Practice/Apply

Play a version of "Simon Says" with children, using such phrases as: *Find your ears, touch your toes, put your hands on your hips, cover your eyes.*

SKILL FINDER

Our Whole Selves, p. T83

Science Link

Have children notice that two of the children on page 27 are missing teeth. Ask children to share whether they have lost any teeth. Explain to them that when baby teeth fall out, new teeth grow to replace them.

MEETING INDIVIDUAL NEEDS

Students Acquiring English

Names for Body Parts Pair children acquiring English with fluent English speakers. Then, have them work together to point to and name their own eyes, ears, noses, and mouths.

Interact with Literature

BIG BOOK

Faces, faces, from all kinds of places.

28

Faces.

30

Reading Strategies

▶ **Summarize**

Explain that one way children can be sure they remember this story is by retelling it in their own words. Ask them what important parts they would need to include to tell this story by themselves. If they have difficulty, have them refer to their journal entries and to page through the book looking for what they missed. Then have them take turns retelling the story to a partner.

Self-Assessment

Ask children to tell about some of the things they could have done if they couldn't summarize the ideas easily. Discuss these questions:

- Did I go back and look at the pictures?
- Did I reread and think about the parts of a face?
- Did I remember important information about what each part of the face can do?

QuickREFERENCE

Phonemic Awareness Review

Say the story words *faces* and *places* and ask children whether these words rhyme. If necessary, remind children that rhyming words have the same last sounds.

MEETING INDIVIDUAL NEEDS
Challenge

Concepts About Print Explain that the words on page 28 all form one sentence. Note that the sentence begins with a capital letter and ends with a period. The commas tell the readers to pause. Reread the sentence with children.

Social Studies

Note the boy holding the soccer ball on page 28. Explain that soccer is a popular sport all over the world. Invite children to name sports they enjoy.

29

31

MEETING INDIVIDUAL NEEDS

Challenge

Invite children to choose their favorite pages from the story. Have each child practice and then read aloud the words, phrases, or sentences on those pages.

32

Interact with Literature

Rereading

Literacy Activity Book, p. 10

faces seeing,

faces hearing,

faces smelling.

Choices for Rereading

Noting Language Patterns

LAB, p.10

Invite children to reread *Faces* with you and note the repetition of the word *faces* on almost every spread.

Then help children note the following pattern as you read the selection again: *Faces talking, faces smelling, faces hearing, faces seeing.*

Have children complete *Literacy Activity Book,* page 10 to practice the language pattern.

Listen and Read!

 Audio Tape for All About Me: *Faces*

Place the Audio Tape and copies of Little Big Book in the Listening Center. Invite children to chime in with the tape as they read the story individually or in small groups.

Listen and Point

 Students Acquiring English
Reread the story asking children to point to the parts of their faces as they are mentioned. For example, when you read *Faces seeing*, children should point to their eyes.

Fill in the Blank

To promote children's confidence in shared reading, read the story again leaving out words for them to fill in where the context suggests what word may come next. (Example: "Faces, faces, all kinds of _____." (faces))

Informal Assessment

Use the Retelling activity to assess children's general understanding of the selection.

Responding

Choices for Responding

Personal Response

Have pairs of children draw detailed pictures of each other's face. Children should take the drawings home to introduce a classmate to members of their family and to talk about the story.

Retelling *Faces*

Have pairs take turns retelling the story. Ask one child to turn the pages of the Little Big Book as the other child looks at the photographs and tells the story.

Just Like Me

Ask children to think about what things they have done that children in *Faces* have done, such as making funny faces or having their face painted. Have them draw a picture of their experience and write, or dictate, a sentence about it. Suggest that they share their drawings with others.

Self-Portraits

Provide children with handheld mirrors and invite them to draw self-portraits. Encourage them to include all the facial features. Then help children label each feature.

Materials
- drawing paper
- handheld mirrors
- crayons

Portfolio Opportunity

Save children's work on Just Like Me as a sample of their responses to the story. Also keep *Literacy Activity Book* page 10 to record their understanding of the story's language pattern.

3

Instruct *and* Integrate

Comprehension

Literacy Activity Book, p. 11

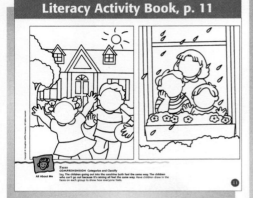

Practice Activities

Categorize and Classify

Extra Support Recall with children that certain photographs in *Faces* were put together on the same page because they were alike in some way. Explain that knowing this plan helps us to enjoy the story. Display pages 14–15 and ask children what kinds of faces were put together on these pages. (funny faces) Then invite children to find pictures of faces in magazines or books that could go with these pictures. Have children share and discuss the pictures they find.

You might want to repeat this procedure with other categories from the story, such as feeling faces, friendly faces, thinking faces, and sleeping faces, or invite pairs or groups of children to pick a category and look for those kinds of pictures.

Materials
● magazines and picture books

Categorize/Classify
LAB, p. 11

Have children complete *Literacy Activity Book,* page 11, for further practice with categorizing and classifying.

Challenge Encourage partners to brainstorm games for sunny days and games for rainy days.

Noting Details in Photographs

Review the story illustrations with children, having them note how the children's expressions in the pictures show how they feel about what they're doing. Ask questions such as the following:

● Does the tulip have a pretty smell? How do you know?

● Is the baby happy?

● How can you tell if the face-painters are having fun?

● Are the children enjoying their ice cream cones? Why do you think so?

Informal Assessment

As children complete the activities, note their ability to categorize and classify, and to identify the names for parts of the body.

Concept Development

Practice Activities

Our Whole Selves

- Display *Faces* and read pages 24–27, inviting children to point to the features on their faces as they are mentioned. (eyes, ears, noses, mouths) Then encourage them to name other facial features they know such as eyelids, teeth, and so on. Explain to children that just like our faces, the rest of our bodies have different parts or features.

- Show children how one child can lie on the paper while another traces around him or her. The partners then trade roles. Then they can cut out both figures.

- Encourage them to color or draw themselves the way they look today.

- As children work, circulate and help them name all the body parts on their tracings. Ask: What part of your body are you coloring now? Where are your legs? Arms? Hands? Feet? How many fingers are on each hand?

- Then children can take turns showing their tracings to the class. Encourage them to make affirming comments about what they see. ("I like the way you drew your hair." "You did a good job with your eyes.")

Extra Support Ask older children or parent helpers to work with children to make their body tracings. Encourage them to help the children name the parts of the body as they help children trace and cut out their figures.

Literacy Activity Book, p.12

Materials
- large newsprint paper for each child
- crayons, scissors

Parts of the Body
LAB, p. 12

Have children complete Literacy Activity Book, page 12, to practice identifying the parts of the body.

Name the Feature

- Prepare milk carton dice with different facial features on each surface.

- Provide pairs with a die and large paper with a large blank face drawn on it.

- Have children take turns rolling the die, naming the feature that turns up, and drawing that feature on the blank face.

Portfolio Opportunity

To have a record of children's ability to recognize and identify the names for parts of the body, save *Literacy Activity Book* page 12.

Instruct
and
Integrate

Concepts About Print

Practice Activities

Right Side Up

Extra Support Display various theme-related books at the front of the room, some turned upside down, or sideways. Then invite volunteers to choose a book and demonstrate for the class how to hold the book right side up and how to turn the pages.

Where Does a Book Begin and End?

Using the same books from the Right Side Up Activity, invite volunteers to show where the book begins and where it ends. If necessary, remind children that the front cover is the beginning of the book and the back cover is the end.

Where Does a Page Begin and End?

Challenge Tell children that each page of a book has a beginning and an end and that as we read the words on each page, we go from the first word to the last word. Have volunteers choose a book, open it to a page with text and ask them to point out where they will begin reading and stop reading on this page. Then read the page aloud sweeping your hand under the words from left to right. Repeat this procedure with several other pages.

Informal Assessment

As children complete the activities, note their ability to hold books, turn pages, and scan print correctly. Also observe how well they listen to and follow directions.

Listening

Practice Activities

Following Directions

- Ask children to listen carefully and follow your instructions. Explain that you will say each direction twice.

- Give instructions that encourage them to identify different parts of their bodies. Say each direction twice and allow time for children to complete each before moving to the next. Some sample instructions might be:

  Close your eyes.

  Open your eyes.

  Touch your nose.

  Raise your arms over your head.

  Clap your hands.

  Touch your feet.

  Touch your ears.

  Students Acquiring English You might pair up children who are learning English with native speakers and have them face each other during this activity.

What Do You Hear?

Display page 25 of the Big Book and invite children to name this part of the body and to recall what we use it for. (ear, hearing or listening) Invite children to use their sense of hearing to listen for different noises in the classroom, on the playground, or at home. Have them choose one of these locations and record the sounds they hear by drawing a picture of the person, animal, or object that makes the noise.

Listen and Read!

 Audio Tape for All About Me: *Faces*

Place copies of the Little Big Book *Faces* along with the Audio Tape in the Reading/Listening Center. Have children match the spoken words to print by pointing to each word as the narrator reads.

3

Instruct *and* Integrate

Independent Reading & Writing

First Day of School
illustrated by Jan Palmer

This story provides an independent reading experience with theme content and concepts.

INTERACTIVE LEARNING

Independent Reading
Watch Me Read

Preview and Predict	• Display *First Day of School.* Point to and read the title and illustrator's name.
	• Briefly discuss the cover illustration with children, allowing time for children to predict what this story might be about and to comment on how they felt on the first day of school.
	• Explain that this is a story without words, and that children can tell the story by looking at the pictures.
Telling the Story	• The wordless book, *First Day of School,* will provide children with an independent book experience. Encourage children to tell the story to themselves as they look at each picture to see if their predictions about *First Day of School* are correct.
	• After completing the story, ask:
	How was the girl's first day of school like your own?
	How was her first day of school different?
Choices for Rereading	• **Tell It to a Friend** Encourage children to take turns telling the story to classmates or to adults in the classroom.
	• **Concept Review** Have children look at the pictures and tell the story again noting how the girl's feelings change during the day and how her parents feel. Encourage them to use some of the feeling words they have learned.
Choices For Responding	• **Personal Response** Invite children to tell what they liked best about the story. Encourage them to draw a picture in their journals to show their favorite part.
	• **Act It Out** Invite children to act out different scenes from the story. Encourage them to use dialogue, facial expressions, and gestures to help the audience understand how each character is feeling.

Informal Assessment

Observe children to see if they can
- Find books they enjoy reading
- Handle books correctly
- Select their own writing topics
- Make an attempt to write on their own

Student-Selected Reading

Books for the Library Corner

Display the Books for the Library Corner suggested in the Bibliography on pages T6-T7 in an accessible place for children. Encourage children to explore these titles during scheduled reading time as well as independent leisure time.

Sharing and Reflecting

Schedule times when children can share favorite stories. Encourage children to be creative as they share their excitement over a book they have listened to or read.

- Pictures of important scenes can be displayed during the retelling of a story.
- Dressing up as the main character will make a retelling more dramatic.

Student-Selected Writing

Sharing Ideas

Writing activities that children initiate for their own purposes are usually the most motivating. If children seem to be having difficulty coming up with any of their own ideas, allow peers to share some of their ideas or encourage them to write a new version of a story they have listened to or read.

Exploring Letter Forms

Provide various mediums and utensils—salt, sand, finger paints, markers, pencils, pens for children to practice writing and forming letters.

Books for Independent Reading

Encourage children to choose their own books. They might choose one of the following titles.

First Day of School
illustrated by Jan Palmer

ABC and You
by Eugenie Fernandes

Faces
by Shelley Rotner
and Ken Kreisler

Have pairs of children share the reading of these. Some children may be able to read them independently.

See the theme Bibliography on pages T6-T7 for more theme-related books for independent reading.

Ideas for Independent Writing

Encourage children to write on self-selected topics. For those who need help getting started, suggest one of the following activities:

- An alphabet letter **picture book**
- **Labeling** parts of the body or face
- A **name card** to put on a desktop or cubby
- A **week timeline** to draw or list feelings on each day

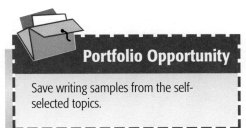

Portfolio Opportunity

Save writing samples from the self-selected topics.

3

Instruct
and
Integrate

Oral Language

Choices for Oral Language

Tips for Talking

- one person talks at a time
- listen to the person talking
- look at the person talking
- take turns talking

Faces Talking

Display page 8 of *Faces* and read the phrase with children. Then write Tips for Talking on the board. Read them and discuss them with children. Then invite two volunteers to the front of the classroom to have a conversation together. If necessary, provide them with a topic. Have the others note whether they follow the tips for talking. Repeat with other volunteers.

The Telephone Game

Display page 8 of *Faces* and ask children to tell you what the girl is doing. (whispering) Invite children to play a game where they will have to whisper. Have them sit in a circle with you. Explain that you are going to whisper a sentence to the child at your right, and that children are to pass it along by whispering it to the next person all the way around the circle. The last child should say the message aloud.

What Else Can Faces Do?

Read pages 6 –11 and have children identify the words that tell what the faces are doing. (talking, smelling, hearing, seeing, thinking, sleeping) Have children suggest other words the author could have used to tell what faces can do. Record children's suggestions in a word web on chart paper.

Tear-and-Take Story

Home Connection Have children remove *Literacy Activity Book,* page 13, fold it to make a book, and tell the story. Then suggest that they take their books home and tell them to family members.

Just Right for Me

Informal Assessment

As children tell the Tear-and-Take story, note how easily they use words to describe what's happening in the pictures. Also observe how well they recall body parts and label them on their drawing.

Writing

Choices for Writing

Body Diagrams

Display one of the children's body tracings with the parts of the body labeled. Then invite interested children to draw themselves and label the parts of the body using the labeled body tracing for reference. Some children might like to put this diagram in their All About Me Books. (See the Ongoing Project, page T12.)

Materials

- Body Tracing from *Our Whole Selves* (See Concept Development, page T83)

My Eyes Are Brown

Talk about children's eye colors with them. Then make the following sentence strip and read it to them:

> My eyes are _____.

Invite children to copy it and fill in the blank. Put colors labeled with color words in the Language/Writing Center for children to use if they wish. Children might like to copy their sentences into their All About Me Books. (See the Ongoing Project, page T12.)

Me and My Name

Review some of the ways that the children in all of the theme selections were special. (feelings, names, faces, what they liked to do) Have children write their names on paper banners and decorate them in a way that tells something about how they are special—such as their face, something they like very much, a favorite food, something they're always saying or doing. Invite children to write or dictate any messages they may want on their banners. Then display the banners in the classroom.

Instruct *and* Integrate

Cross-Curricular Activities

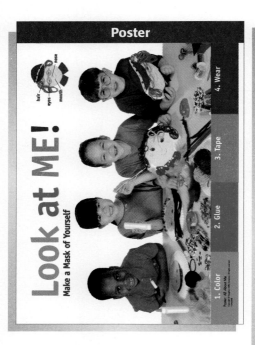

Poster

Choices for Math

Hearing Patterns

Remind children that they hear with their ears. Ask them to close their eyes while you model a simple pattern–clap, snap fingers, clap, snap fingers. Invite them to join in. Then have children suggest and model another pattern.

Counting

Review page 8 of *Faces* and explain that you are going to whisper certain instructions for them to follow.

- Whisper instructions to a child such as "Go to the Writing Center and bring back pencils–one for you and one for Mario." Let the child perform the actions while the others watch carefully. Ask: What did you see? Can you tell about what just happened? How many things were carried?

- Repeat the procedure with different children, varying the destination, the objects, and the number.

Art

Look At Me!

- Invite children to create their own self-portrait masks.

- Display the Look at Me! poster and read it with children.

- Ask them to identify the features they want to put on their masks.

- Allow time for them to explore the art materials and share ideas for decorating their masks.

- Then let children decorate and wear their masks.

Materials
- Look At Me! poster
- white paper plates, 7"
- markers, yarn, paste, paint, and other art supplies

Social Studies

Costumes Around the World

Display pages 28–31 of the *Faces* and explain that people from different countries sometimes wear costumes or clothing that are special to them or to the place they live. Ask children to share their feelings about the different types of dress shown on these pages. Then display and discuss pictures from books and magazines of clothing from around the world. You may want to talk about how things like climate affect how people dress.

Science

The Five Senses

Familiarize children with the terms that describe the five senses —*taste, touch, hearing, smell, and sight*— and the parts of the body used for each sense. Then invite children to explore different objects using their senses.

- Provide each child with a different object.
- Ask them to use their senses to learn more about the object.

Note: Be sure to eliminate taste or smell from their exploration if it is not safe.

- Have children record what they learn about their object.
- Ask volunteers to share their findings. You might help them by asking: What did you learn using your sense of sight? hearing? taste? touch? smell?

Materials
- various natural or found objects or food—preferably make available items with which children will be unfamiliar.

Theme Assessment Wrap-Up

ASSESSMENT

Reflecting/Self-Assessment

Copy the chart below to distribute to children. Ask them which stories in the theme they liked best. Then discuss what was easy for them and what was more difficult as they read the selections and completed the activities. Have children put a check mark under either *Easy* or *Hard*.

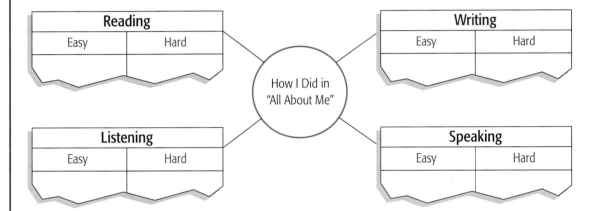

Reading	
Easy	Hard

Writing	
Easy	Hard

How I Did in "All About Me"

Listening	
Easy	Hard

Speaking	
Easy	Hard

Monitoring Literacy Development

There will be many opportunities to observe and evaluate children's literacy development. As children participate in literacy activities, note whether each child has a beginning, a developing, or a proficient understanding of reading, writing, and language concepts. The Observation Checklists, which can be used for recording and evaluating this information, appear in the *Teacher's Assessment Handbook.* They are comprised of the following:

Concepts About Print and Book Handling Behaviors

- Concepts about print
- Book handling

Emergent Reading Behaviors

- Responding to literature
- Storybook rereading
- Decoding strategies

Emergent Writing Behaviors

- Writing
- Stages of temporary spelling

Oral Language Behaviors

- Listening attentively
- Listening for information
- Listening to directions
- Listening to books
- Speaking/language development
- Participating in conversations and discussions

Retelling Behaviors

- Retelling a story
- Retelling informational text

Portfolio Opportunity

Invite children to save one piece of work that they did during "All About Me."

Choices for Assessment

Informal Assessment

Review the Observation Checklists and observation notes to determine:

- Did children's responses during and after reading indicate comprehension of the selections?

- How well did children understand the skills presented in this theme? Which skills should be reviewed and practiced in the next theme?

- Did children enjoy the cooperative activities related to the major theme concept?

Formal Assessment

Select formal tests that meet your classroom needs:

- *Kindergarten Literacy Survey*
- Theme Skills Test for "All About Me"

See the *Teacher's Assessment Handbook* for guidelines for administering tests and using answer keys and children's sample papers.

Portfolio Assessment

Introducing Portfolios to the Class

Explain to children that their portfolios are a place to keep samples of their work for the year. Kindergarten portfolios are shared by the teacher and the children; however, at this level the teacher usually does most of the selecting of work to place in the portfolio. By looking at their work, children will be able to see how they have grown and changed over time. In addition, there are often teacher observation checklists and notes. Children can be encouraged to place work in their portfolios, but it is not expected.

As a first step, have children create folders in which to keep their special work. Have them decorate their portfolios. Choose something for them to place in the portfolio that first day. Be sure to date every entry. You may want to provide a date stamp for children to use before they place work in their portfolios.

Managing Assessment
Evaluating Children at the Beginning of the Year

Question: How can I evaluate kindergarten children at the beginning of the year?

Answer: Try these suggestions:

- Use the *Kindergarten Literacy Survey* to assess children's abilities with shared reading, concepts about print, book handling, phonemic awareness, letter names, and emergent writing.

- After reading a story aloud to children, ask them to draw a picture to answer a particular question. Encourage them to write about their pictures. Use this activity to evaluate listening comprehension and emergent writing.

- Have children create a self-portrait to note their fine motor coordination.

For more information on this and other topics, see the *Teacher's Assessment Handbook.*

Celebrating the Theme

Choices for Celebrating

Materials
- **Read Aloud Book:** *On Monday When It Rained*
- **Big Books:** *ABC and You; Faces*
- **WATCH ME READ:** *First Day of School*

Book Talk

Display the different books and ask children to talk about which book is their favorite and why. Then group children according to their favorite story and give the appropriate book to each group. Invite children to take turns retelling the story.

See the **Houghton Mifflin Internet** resources for additional theme-related activities.

Self-Assessment

Have children meet in small groups to discuss what they learned in the theme. Use the following prompts to foster their discussion:

- Which selection in the theme did you like best?
- Name as many letter names, feeling words, and parts of the body as you can.

Theme Talk

Invite children to share what they've learned during the theme:

- Review the letter names and discuss how knowing these names willl help them to read. Children may also want to discuss what they learned about rhyming words, feelings, and different parts of the body.

- Invite children to share their favorite writing projects such as their All About Me books, their body diagrams, or the class alphabet story.

- Encourage children to name ways they are special—feelings, facial features, names, and so on. Then invite them to sing the theme song "I Am Special, I Am Me." (See Teacher's Handbook, page H12.)

An Art Show

Create an art display of children's work as well as theme posters and books. Invite other classes to view the show.

Ideas for the Art Show:

- Hang children's body tracings on a line and have volunteers point to and name the different body parts.

- Have volunteers stand near the Look at Us board and explain the display.

- Have a station set up where children help visitors design their own name tags or banners.

- Have an "art in action" exhibit. Have volunteers hold up the story retelling frame and display different facial expressions to demonstrate the feeling words they have learned.

- Prepare snacks that are in the shape of different letters of the alphabet.

Color Is Everywhere

Table of Contents

THEME: Color Is Everywhere

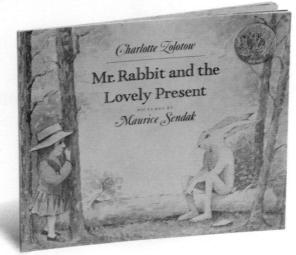

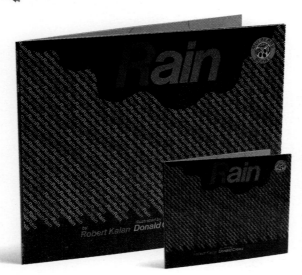

Bibliography
Books for the Library Corner

 Multicultural

 Science/Health

 Math

 Social Studies

 Music

 Art

Growing Colors
by Bruce McMillan
Lothrop 1988 (32p) Mulberry 1994 paper
Photographs reveal the beautiful colors in garden fruits and vegetables.

Close-Up Colors
Snapshot 1995 (20p)
Children pull tabs to discover that one close-up color image changes into another.

Colors
by Pascale De Bourgoing
Scholastic 1991 (24p)
See-through pages change the pictures in this primer about color.

Counting Wildflowers
by Bruce McMillan
Mulberry paper 1995 (32p)
Photographs of twenty brilliant wildflowers introduce colors and counting.

A Fishy Color Story
by Joanne and David Wylie
Childrens 1983 (32p) paper
Bold illustrations of fish illustrate the concept of colors. **Available in Spanish as Un cuento curioso de colores.**

The Colors
by Monique Felix
Creative Education (32p) 1992
A mouse eats her way into a book and has an adventure with color. (Wordless)

Color Zoo
by Lois Ehlert
Lippincott 1989 (32p)
Geometric shapes and different colors combine to create nine zoo animals.

My Blue Boat
by Chris L. Demarest
Harcourt 1995 (32p)
Playing in the bathtub with her blue boat, a girl imagines an adventurous ocean voyage.

A Child's Book of Art: Great Pictures, First Words
by Lucy Micklethwait
Dorling Kindersley 1993 (64p)
Children learn about color and art appreciation by looking at works of art.

Colors Everywhere
by Tana Hoban
Greenwillow 1995 (32p)
Stunning photographs reveal the myriad colors found everywhere (Wordless)

Planting a Rainbow
by Lois Ehlert
Harcourt 1988 (32p) also paper
Planting a garden of flowers, a child learns about the colors of the rainbow.

The Color Box
by Dayle Ann Dodds
Little 1992 (32p)
Readers follow Alexander the monkey inside a box and through a world of colors.

Finding Red, Finding Yellow
by Betsy Imershein
Harcourt 1989 (32p)
Readers discover red and yellow in familiar objects in the world around them. (Wordless)

Red Bear
Bodel Rikys
Dial 1992 (32p)
Red Bear has a busy day full of color and adventure.

Blue Bug's Book of Colors
by Virginia Poulet
Childrens 1981 (32p)
Blue Bug discovers that mixing two colors together creates a new one. **Available in Spanish as El libro de colores de Azulín.**

Of Colors and Things
by Tana Hoban
Greenwillow 1989 (24p)
Groupings of familiar items invite children to identify colors, shapes, and objects. (Wordless)

Books for Teacher Read Aloud

All the Colors of the Earth
by Sheila Hamanaka
Morrow 1994 (32p)
A poetic celebration of the diversity of the world's children.

Samuel Todd's Book of Great Colors
by E. L. Konigsburg
Atheneum 1990 (32p)
A young boy observes how color illuminates the world around him.

El señor Conejo y el hermoso regalo (Mr. Rabbit and the Lovely Present)
by Charlotte Zolotow
Text in Spanish.

Mouse Paint
by Ellen Stoll Walsh
Harcourt 1989 (32p) also paper
Three white mice experiment with jars of red, yellow, and blue paint.

Harold and the Purple Crayon
by Robert Kraus
Harper 1955 (64p) also paper
A boy out for a walk draws adventures for himself with a purple crayon. **Available in Spanish as Harold y el lápiz color morado.**

White Is the Moon
by Valerie Greeley
Macmillan 1991 (32p)
The theme of color links verse and scenes from nature that take the reader through a day.

What Is Color?
by Christina Rossetti
Harper 1992 (40p)
A well-known poem about color is paired with pictures of familiar objects.

A Rainbow of My Own
by Don Freeman
Viking 1966 (32p) Puffin 1978
A little boy longs to have a rainbow all his own.

Colors
by Shirley Hughes
Lothrop 1986 (24p)
Rhyming verse introduces colors in objects and places.

Color Dance
★ *by Ann Jonas*
Greenwillow 1989 (32p)
Dancers waving scarves demonstrate different combinations of color.

Books for Shared Reading

Hide and Seek in the Yellow House
by Agatha Rose
Viking 1992 (32p) Puffin 1995 paper
In a yellow house, a mother cat searches for her kitten.

Brown Bear, Brown Bear, What Do You See?
by Bill Martin, Jr.
Holt 1992 (32p)
A variety of animals answer the question "What do you see?" in a playful book about color.

The Green Queen
by Nick Sharratt
Candlewick 1992 (24p)
The green queen wears her many-colored scarf when she goes out for a walk.

Freight Train
by Donald Crews
Greenwillow 1978 (32p) also paper
A freight train of colored cars brings the reader on an exciting ride.

Red Is Best
by Kathy Stinson
Annick 1982 (32p) Firefly 1992 paper
A girl explains why her favorite clothes are red. **Available in Spanish as *El rojo es el mejor.***

Mary Wore Her Red Dress and Henry Wore His Green Sneakers
🎸 *by Merle Peek*
Clarion 1985 (32p) also paper
Katy's animal friends dress in different colors to go to her birthday party.

I Went Walking
by Sue Williams
Harcourt 1989 (32p) also paper
A young child goes walking and identifies animals including a brown horse and a pink pig. **Available in Spanish as *Salí de paseo.***

Yellow Ball
★ *by Molly Bang*
Morrow 1991 (24p)
A little boy's yellow ball drifts out to sea and washes up on a distant shore.

Technology Resources

Computer Software
Internet See the Houghton Mifflin **Internet** resources for additional bibliographic entries and theme-related activities.

Video Cassettes
Freight Train *by Donald Crews.* Am. Sch. Pub.

Harold and the Purple Crayon *by Robert Kraus.* Listening Library

The Red Carpet *by Rex Parkin.* Weston Woods

Audio Cassettes
A Rainbow of My Own *by Don Freeman.* Live Oak Media

Mr. Rabbit and the Lovely Present *by Charlotte Zolotow.* Am. Sch. Pub.

Filmstrips
Colors and Shapes. Nat'l Geo

Stories About Colors. Am. Sch. Pub.

The Yellow Umbrella *by Henrik Drescher.* Am. Sch. Pub.

Roses Are Red. Are Violets Blue? Am. Sch. Pub.

AV addresses are in Teacher's Handbook, pages H15–H16.

Theme at a Glance

Reading/Listening Center

Selections	Comprehension Skills and Strategies	Phonemic Awareness	Concept Development	Concepts About Print
Mr. Rabbit and the Lovely Present	✓ Inferences: making predictions, T113, T120 The birthday party, T120 Speculating about picnic scene, T120 Reading strategies, T110, T112, T116 **Rereading and responding,** T118-T119	✓ Rhyming words, T115, T121 Recognizing rhymes, T121 Nursery rhymes, T121	Color, T117	
Rain	✓ Story structure (beginning), T131 Story structure (middle), T133 Story structure (end), T139 Reading strategies, T130, T132, T136, T138 Story mural, T142 Categorizing colors, T142 Identifying beginning, middle, end, T142 **Rereading and responding,** T140-T141		Color, T135 Weather, T143 The colors of the rainbow, T143 How to make a gray cloud, T143	✓ Directionality, T137 Directional rules, T144 Rainbow letters, T144 Scratchboard art, T144
Who Said Red?	✓ Inferences: drawing conclusions, T167, T172 Concluding questions, T172 Drawing conclusions, T172 Reading strategies, T154, T156, T158, T164, T166, T168 **Rereading and responding,** T170-T171		Color, T159, T173 Color wheels, T173 Questions and answers, T173	✓ Directionality/return sweep, T161 Fun with sentence strips, T174 Favorite colors, T174 Return sweep, T161

✓ *Indicates Tested Skills. See page T103 for assessment options.*

Language/Writing Center   Cross-Curricular Center

Listening	Oral Language	Writing	Content Areas
	Guessing game, T122 Presents, T122 Identifying vegetables, T122 Colors of birds, T122	Fruit salad recipe, T123 A card, T123 Colors of the sky, T123	**Math:** a birthday calendar, T124; favorite color graph, T124 **Science:** investigating seeds, T124; investigating butterflies and caterpillars, T125 **Art:** making play dough fruits, T125
Listening to the audio tape, T145 Playing I spy, T145 A story from you!, T145 Japanese rain song, T145	A play, T146 Dramatic play, T146 Weather words, T146	Class story, T129 Writing about weather, T147 Making a rainbow, T147 Writing a poem, T147	**Science:** investigating water, T148; the habits of water, T148 **Art:** making a movie, T148; making flowers, T149 **Social Studies:** learning about roads, T149
Listening to the audio tape, T175 Rhymes, T175 Listen to a story, T175 Rules for listening, T175	Colors and feelings, T178 A play about colors, T178 New story, T178	Class story, T153 Making a big book, T179 Self portraits, T179 A present, T179 Story ideas, T177	**Music:** learning "Mary Wore Her Red Dress," T180 **Art:** painting techniques, T180; designing kites, T180 **Math:** making a color graph, T181 **Social Studies:** learning about the color red, T181

Meeting Individual Needs

Key to Meeting Individual Needs

 Students Acquiring English

Activities and notes throughout the lesson plans offer strategies to help children understand the selections and lessons.

 **Challenge**

Challenge activities and notes throughout the lesson plans suggest additional activities to stimulate critical and creative thinking.

 Extra Support

Activities and notes throughout the lesson plans offer additional strategies to help children experience success.

Managing Instruction

Developing Active Listening Skills

Teach children to give their complete attention to a designated speaker by

- Signaling for complete attention: three claps.

- All turning toward the person who is supposed to be talking.

- Opening ears to listen and closing mouths.

- Keeping hands quiet by placing them palms down on the table or folding them on their lap.

Once the routine is learned, enable children to be successful by keeping the time frame for active learning to short, manageable segments.

For further information on this and other Managing Instruction topics, see the *Professional Development Handbook.*

Performance Standards

During this theme, children will

- *read about colors and learn color names*
- *monitor and evaluate their reading*
- *apply comprehension skills: Making Predictions, Identifying Story Structure (Beginning, Middle, End), Drawing Conclusions*
- *retell or summarize each selection*
- *apply return sweep*
- *identify rhymes*
- *apply directionality*
- *write a story*

Students Acquiring English	Challenge	Extra Support
Develop Key Concepts Children focus on Key Concepts through picture previews, making charts and graphs, and playing matching and sorting games.	**Apply Critical Thinking** This theme offers opportunities to apply critical thinking. These include making predictions and drawing conclusions.	**Enhance Self-Confidence** With extra support provided for reading and responding to the literature, children will see themselves as active members of the reading community.
Expand Vocabulary Children use context and picture clues, discuss meanings, and model definitions. Children expand their vocabulary to include pronouns and words within a given category, adjectives, and color words.	**Explore Real-life Situations** Activities that motivate further exploration include examining fruit seeds, conducting weather experiments, and designing a kite.	**Receive Increased Instructional Time on Skills** Practice activities in the Reading/Listening Center provide support with making predictions, drawing conclusions, and story structure.
Act as a Resource Children are asked to share "Happy Birthday" in native languages and discuss proper forms of address.	**Engage in Creative Thinking** Opportunities for creative expression include dramatizing a story, making a rainbow, investigating background details, and writing a poem.	**Provide Independent Reading** Children can also take home the Tear-and-Take stories in their *Literacy Activity Books* and the black-and-white versions of the WATCH ME READ titles to read.

Additional Resources

Invitaciones

Develop bi-literacy with this integrated reading/language arts program in Spanish. Provides authentic literature and real-world resources from Spanish-speaking cultures.

Language Support

Translations of Big Books in Chinese, Hmong, Khmer, and Vietnamese. *Teacher's Booklet* provides instructional support in English.

Students Acquiring English Handbook

Guidelines, strategies, and additional instruction for students acquiring English

Planning for Assessment

Informal Assessment

Observation Checklists

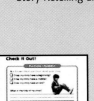

- Concepts About Print/Book Handling
- Responding to Literature and Decoding Behaviors and Strategies
- Writing Behaviors and Stages of Temporary Spelling
- Listening and Speaking Behaviors
- Story Retelling and Rereading

Literacy Activity Book

Recommended pages for children's portfolios:
- Phonemic Awareness: Rhyming Words, p. 17
- Personal Response, p. 18
- Comprehension: Story Structure, p. 20
- Language Patterns, p. 23
- Concept Development: Colors (Objects), p. 25

Retellings-Oral/Written

- *Teacher's Assessment Handbook*

Formal Assessment

Kindergarten Literacy Survey

Evaluates children's literacy development. Provides holistic indicator of children's ability with
- Shared Reading/Constructing Meaning
- Concepts About Print
- Phonemic Awareness
- Emergent Writing

Kindergarten Literacy Survey

Managing Assessment

Observation Checklists

Question How can I manage to record information on the Observation Checklists?

Answer The Observation Checklists can help you keep track of informal observations you make throughout the year. There are several checklists available in the Teacher's Assessment Handbook—Concepts About Print, Book Handling, Emergent Reading, Emergent Writing, Oral Language, and Retelling. These tips keep the checklists simple to use:

- There are individual and group checklist forms. Use the group form to monitor most children. Use the individual form for children who are a focus of concern.

- Some teachers keep a checklist on a clipboard and make notes as they teach. Others take a moment at the end of the day to reflect and record their observations. Experiment to find the way that works best for you.

- Kindergarten checklists are designed to be used throughout the year as children develop. Therefore, you won't need to record observations very often—some teachers find once a month sufficient.

For more information on this and other topics, see the *Teacher's Assessment Handbook*.

Portfolio Assessment

The portfolio icon signals portfolio opportunities throughout the theme.

Additional Portfolio Tips:
- Selecting Materials for the Portfolio, T183

Launching the Theme

See the Houghton Mifflin **Internet** resources for additional activities.

Audio Tape for Color Is Everywhere: *"What Is Pink?"*

See the *Home/Community Connections Booklet* for theme-related materials.

INTERACTIVE LEARNING

Warm-Up

Sharing the Theme Poem

- Ask several children to name their favorite colors. Then mention that you are going to read a poem about colors.

- Play the audio tape for "What Is Pink?" for children. As they listen, hold up a crayon or color sample for each color: pink, red, blue, white, yellow, green, violet, orange.

- Give the color samples to children. Invite them to name things that are each color as you ask: "What is pink?" "What is red?" and so on.

- Play the audio tape again, and have children hold up the appropriate color.

Interactive Bulletin Board

Color Is Everywhere

This bulletin board reinforces the concept of color.

- Prepare some large tagboard letters to spell *Color Is Everywhere.*

- Have children color each tagboard letter.

- Attach the letters to the bulletin board; ask children to name the letters as you put them up.

- During the theme, encourage children to add color names, together with pictures of objects associated with each color, to the bulletin board.

Ongoing Project

Art Gallery

Children will be celebrating color through a variety of art media all during this theme. Provide another large space with walls and shelves so children can display their artwork in their very own gallery. From time to time, invite family members and other children in the school to visit the gallery.

Portfolio Opportunity

The Portfolio Opportunity icon highlights portfolio opportunities throughout the theme.

Choices for Centers

Creating Centers

Use these activities to create learning centers in the classroom.

Reading/Listening Center

- Rhyme Time, T121
- Story Mural, T142
- Fun with Sentence Strips, T174

Language/Writing Center

- Perfect Presents, T122
- Writing About Weather, T147
- A Play About Colors, T178

Cross-Curricular Center

- Favorite Color Graph, T124
- Water Watch, T148
- Mary Wore Her Red Dress, T180

READ ALOUD

SELECTION:

Mr. Rabbit and the Lovely Present

by Charlotte Zolotow

Other Books by Charlotte Zolotow

I Like to Be Little

Sleepy Book

Something Is Going to Happen

William's Doll

- **Caldecott Honor Books**
- **ALA Notable Children's Books**
- **Best Books for Children**

Selection Summary

When a little girl has nothing to give her mother for her birthday, she asks a rabbit for help. During a playful dialogue of questions and answers, the girl and the rabbit gather four fruits, each a favorite color of the girl's mother, to be the mother's birthday present.

Lesson Planning Guide

	Skill/Strategy Instruction	Meeting Individual Needs	Lesson Resources
1 Introduce *the* Literature *Pacing: 1 day*	**Preparing to Listen and Write** Warm-Up/Build Background, T108 Read Aloud, T108	**Choices for Rereading,** T109 **Challenge,** T109	**Poster** Sing a Rainbow, T108 *Literacy Activity Book* Personal Response, p. 15
2 Interact *with* Literature *Pacing: 1–2 days*	**Reading Strategies** Monitor, T110 Summarize, T110, T112, T116 **Minilessons** ✔ Inferences: Making Predictions, T113 ✔ Rhyming Words, T115 Color, T117	**Students Acquiring English,** T110, T115, T119 **Extra Support,** T111, T113, T114, T116 **Rereading and Responding,** T118–T119	**Letter, Word, and Picture Cards,** T115 **Story Props,** T119, H4 See the Houghton Mifflin **Internet** resources for additional activities.
3 Instruct *and* Integrate *Pacing: 1–2 days*	**Reading/Listening Center** Comprehension, T120 Phonemic Awareness, T121 **Language/Writing Center** Oral Language, T122 Writing, T123 **Cross-Curricular Center** Cross-Curricular Activities, T124–T125	**Extra Support,** T120, T121 **Challenge,** T121, T124 **Students Acquiring English,** T120	*Literacy Activity Book* Comprehension, p. 16 Phonemic Awareness, p. 17 **Poster** Market Colors, T122 **Game:** Color Round the Rhyme, T121, H8 See the Houghton Mifflin **Internet** resources for additional activities.

✔ *Indicates Tested Skills. See page T103 for assessment options.*

1

Introduce *the* Literature

Preparing to Listen and Write

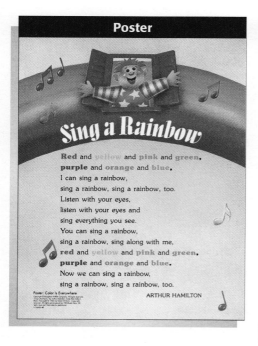

Poster

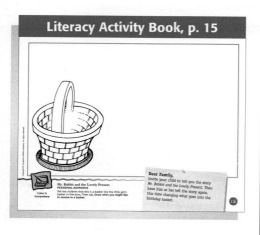

Literacy Activity Book, p. 15

INTERACTIVE LEARNING

Warm-Up/Build Background

Sharing a Song

- Display the poster for "Sing a Rainbow," (see Teacher's Handbook, pages H13–H14, for lyrics) pointing out the rainbow at the top. Encourage children to tell what they know about rainbows. Ask them to name the colors shown in this rainbow, from top to bottom.

- Read aloud the color words in the first two lines of the song. Help children note that the words are printed in the colors they name. Then read or sing the song.

- Read or sing the song again, inviting children to join in—at least on those lines that name color words.

Read Aloud
LAB, p. 15

Preview and Predict

- Display *Mr. Rabbit and the Lovely Present.* Read the title and the names of the author and the illustrator.

- Discuss the picture on the cover. Help children identify Mr. Rabbit. Tell children that the little girl in the picture needs Mr. Rabbit's help. Ask what they think she might need help with. Might she need help finding a present for someone?

Read

Read the story, pausing occasionally for children to predict what they think will happen next and to match their predictions to what actually happens. The following pages are places where you might ask for predictions.

- Page 9: Do you think Mr. Rabbit will suggest something else that's red? What might that be?

- Page 15: What might Mr. Rabbit suggest that's yellow?

- Page 19: What other colors do you think the little girl's mother likes?

As you read, encourage children to ask questions about any parts of the story they don't understand.

Personal Response

Home Connection Invite children to react to the little girl's birthday present for her mother. Then have them complete *Literacy Activity Book,* page 15. Encourage children to take the page home and retell the story to their families.

Noting Picture Details

As you reread the story, help children note which of Mr. Rabbit's suggestions for presents are shown in the illustrations—and which are not. For example:

- The picture on page 11 shows a red roof but does not show a red cardinal.

- The picture on page 17 shows a yellow canary but not a yellow taxicab.

Challenge Children might enjoy drawing their own pictures for some of the items *not* shown in the story's illustrations.

Making Choices

As you reread the story, ask children to tell which of Mr. Rabbit's suggestions they think someone in their own families would like for a present. Encourage children to tell who might like the present and why.

More Choices for Rereading

Rereadings provide varied, repeated experiences with the literature so that children can make its language and content their own. The following rereading choices appear on page T118.

- Reading for Details
- Creating Titles
- Story Language Pattern

Interact with Literature

READ ALOUD

"Mr. Rabbit," said the little girl, "I want help."

"Help, little girl, I'll give you help if I can," said Mr. Rabbit.

"Mr. Rabbit," said the little girl, "it's about my mother."

"Your mother?" said Mr. Rabbit.

"It's her birthday," said the little girl.

"Happy birthday to her then," said Mr. Rabbit. "What are you giving her?"

"That's just it," said the little girl. "That's why I want help. I have nothing to give her."

"Nothing to give your mother on her birthday?" said Mr. Rabbit. "Little girl, you really do want help."

"I would like to give her something that she likes," said the little girl.

"Something that she likes is a good present," said Mr. Rabbit.

Reading Strategies

▶ **Monitor**
Summarize

Teacher Modeling Explain to children that good readers ask themselves if what they are reading makes sense. They also think about the important parts of a story so they can tell the story to someone else. Model these strategies for children.

Think Aloud

As I read *Mr. Rabbit and the Lovely Present,* I'll ask myself if I am understanding what I read. If I am confused, I'll reread or I'll read ahead. I will also think about the important parts of the story. I'll ask myself: Who is this story about? What happens in the story? How does the story end?

Purpose Setting

Suggest that as you read the story again, children think about whom the story is about, what happens in the story, and how the story ends.

Quick REFERENCE

 ★☆★ Multicultural Link

Discuss birthday traditions with children. Have them talk about how their celebrations are both the same and different. Do they give presents? Explain that in some countries, it's a custom to plant a tree on a child's birthday.

 Students Acquiring English

MEETING INDIVIDUAL NEEDS

Point out that the little girl calls the rabbit *Mister* to be polite. The rabbit must seem older, like a grown-up, to the girl. Ask what words children would use—instead of *Mr. Rabbit*—in their own first languages.

Journal

Ask children to draw pictures of presents they have given to family members. Encourage children to try to write the name of the person to whom they gave the gift, as well as their own names, on the picture.

"But what?" said the little girl.
"Yes, what?" said Mr. Rabbit.
"She likes red," said the little girl.
"Red," said Mr. Rabbit. "You can't give her red."
"Something red, maybe," said the little girl.
"Oh, something red," said Mr. Rabbit.
"What is red?" said the little girl.
"Well," said Mr. Rabbit, "there's red underwear."
"No," said the little girl, "I can't give her that."

"There are red roofs," said Mr. Rabbit.
"No, we have a roof," said the little girl. "I don't want to give
her that."
"There are red birds," said Mr. Rabbit, "red cardinals."
"No," said the little girl, "she likes birds in trees."

 Extra Support

Discuss what Mr. Rabbit means when he says, "You can't give her red." Explain that *red* tells what color something is; it's not the name of something you can give someone. Ask children to name something red that could be given to someone.

Science Link

Invite children to find pictures of cardinals and other birds (including canaries and parrots) to show to classmates. Ask children to use color words to describe each bird.

Interact
with
Literature

Reading Strategies

▶ **Summarize**

Teacher Modeling Tell children that the people or animals in a story are called *characters.* Ask them to name the two characters in this story. (Mr. Rabbit, the little girl)

Think Aloud

I know from reading the first part of this story that the little girl is an important character. It's her mother's birthday, and she has no present for her mother. So she asks Mr. Rabbit for help. He's the other important character in this story.

Discuss with children how Mr. Rabbit helps the little girl find something red for her mother.

On a piece of chart paper, draw a few red apples and print the words *red apples.* Continue to add items to the chart as you reread the story with children. Save the chart to help children summarize the story. (See page T116)

"There are red fire engines," said Mr. Rabbit.
"No," said the little girl, "she doesn't like fire engines."
"Well," said Mr. Rabbit, "there are apples."
"Good," said the little girl. "That's good. She likes apples.
But I need something else."

"What else does she like?" said Mr. Rabbit.
"Well, she likes yellow," said the little girl.
"Yellow," said Mr. Rabbit. "You can't give her yellow."
"Something yellow, maybe," said the little girl.
"Oh, something yellow," said Mr. Rabbit.
"What is yellow?" said the little girl.

Quick**REFERENCE**

Social Studies Link

Ask if children know what fire engines are for. Discuss why the girl's mother might not like fire engines. (Perhaps she doesn't like the loud siren that fire engines make when they are going to put out a fire.)

Science Link

Direct attention to the picture on page 13. Point out that apples are fruits that grow on trees. Ask if children have ever helped to pick apples. Encourage those who have to share their experiences.

"Well," said Mr. Rabbit, "there are yellow taxicabs."
"I'm sure she doesn't want a taxicab," said the little girl.
"The sun is yellow," said Mr. Rabbit.
"But I can't give her the sun," said the little girl, "though I
  would if I could."
"A canary bird is yellow," said Mr. Rabbit.
"She likes birds in trees," the little girl said.

"That's right, you told me," said Mr. Rabbit. "Well, butter is
  yellow. Does she like butter?"
"We have butter," said the little girl.
"Bananas are yellow," said Mr. Rabbit.
"Oh, good. That's good," said the little girl. "She likes bananas.
  I need something else, though."

Comprehension

Inferences: Making Predictions

Teach/Model

Remind children that so far in the story, the little girl has chosen two things for her mother's present: red apples and yellow bananas. Reread the last sentence on page 18. Then model for children how they might predict what will happen next.

Think Aloud

The little girl's mother likes red and yellow, which are both colors. She also likes apples and bananas, which are both fruits. The little girl says she needs something else. I would guess that she will choose another color her mother likes; then she will choose a fruit of that color.

Ask children how they might predict that for something green, the girl will choose pears rather than parrots. (Pears are another kind of fruit.)

Practice/Apply

Ask children to draw pictures of other things the girl might choose for her mother's present. Children can use crayons to show color; their pictures should be of fruits.

Inferences: Making
Predictions, p. T120

Minilesson: Theme 5

 Extra Support

Discuss what the girl means when she says, "We have butter." Elicit that she means her family already has butter at home. Ask children where they might look to see if they have butter at home. Ask if children know what butter is made from. (cream)

Social Studies Link

Discuss how taxicabs help people get from place to place. Ask if children have ever ridden in a taxi. Ask them to tell what it was like.

Science Link

Explain that bananas grow on trees—but not in our country. Banana trees grow in places where it's very hot and wet. (We get most of our bananas from Latin America.)

Interact
with
Literature

READ ALOUD

"What else does she like?" said Mr. Rabbit.

"She likes green," said the little girl.

"Green," said Mr. Rabbit. "You can't give her green."

"Something green, maybe," said the little girl.

"Emeralds," said the rabbit. "Emeralds make a lovely gift."

"I can't afford an emerald," said the little girl.

"Parrots are green," said Mr. Rabbit, "but she likes birds in trees."

"No," said the little girl, "parrots won't do."

"Peas and spinach," said Mr. Rabbit. "Peas are green. Spinach is green."

"No," said the little girl. "We have those for dinner all the time."

"Caterpillars," said Mr. Rabbit. "Some of them are very green."

"She doesn't care for caterpillars," the little girl said.

"How about pears?" said Mr. Rabbit. "Bartlett pears?"

"The very thing," said the little girl. "That's the very thing. Now I have apples and bananas and pears, but I need something else."

QuickREFERENCE

MEETING INDIVIDUAL NEEDS

Extra Support

Explain that *emeralds* and *sapphires* are gems, or precious stones, used in making jewelry. Emeralds are green and sapphires are blue.

"What else does she like?" said Mr. Rabbit.
"She likes blue," the little girl said.
"Blue. You can't give her blue," said Mr. Rabbit.
"Something blue, maybe," said the little girl.
"Lakes are blue," said the rabbit.
"But I can't give her a lake, you know," said the little girl.

"Stars are blue."
"I can't give her stars," the little girl said, "but I would if I could."
"Sapphires make a lovely gift," said Mr. Rabbit.
"But I can't afford sapphires, either," said the little girl.
"Bluebirds are blue, but she likes birds in trees," said Mr. Rabbit.
"Right," said the little girl.
"How about blue grapes?" said Mr. Rabbit.

Social Studies Link

Help children find the lake in the picture on page 25. Mention that this lake may be small, like a pond, or just one end of a larger lake. Ask if anyone has ever gone swimming or boating at a lake. What was the lake like?

MEETING INDIVIDUAL NEEDS
Students Acquiring English

If children seem confused, explain that when the little girl says she *can't afford* an emerald, she means that she doesn't have enough money to buy one. Point out that real emeralds are very expensive to buy.

Phonemic Awareness
Rhyming Words

Teach/Model

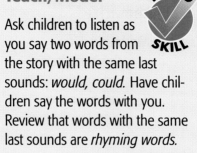

Ask children to listen as you say two words from the story with the same last sounds: *would, could.* Have children say the words with you. Review that words with the same last sounds are *rhyming words*.

Display these Picture Cards:

boat   leaf   goat

Help children name the pictures. Then ask which two picture names rhyme. (boat, goat) Repeat with other Picture Cards, as necessary.

Practice/Apply

Ask children to listen for rhyming words as you say three words. After you say each set of words, ask: "Which *two* words rhyme?" Say these words:

- red, bed, roof
- sun, pear, fun
- lake, girl, rake

Materials
- Picture Cards: *boat, leaf, goat*

SKILL FINDER Rhyme Time, p. T121

READ ALOUD

"Yes," said the little girl. "That is good, very good. She likes grapes. Now I have apples and pears and bananas and grapes."

"That makes a good gift," said Mr. Rabbit. "All you need now is a basket."

"I have a basket," said the little girl.

So she took her basket and she filled it with the green pears and the yellow bananas and the red apples and the blue grapes. It made a lovely present.

Reading Strategies

▶ Summarize

Teacher Modeling Display the chart showing the fruits the girl has chosen for her mother. (See p. T112.) Point to the items on the chart as you model for children how to summarize the story.

Think Aloud

The girl wanted a present for her mother. She asked for Mr. Rabbit's help. He helped her choose red apples, yellow bananas, green pears, and blue grapes. The girl put the fruit in a basket for her mother.

You might ask children if they would like to try to summarize the story now. Refer them to the chart to help them recall the items. Then ask if children think the story could happen in real life. Elicit that while a girl *could* plan a birthday present for her mother, she could not talk with a rabbit.

"Thank you for your help, Mr. Rabbit," said the little girl.

"Not at all," said Mr. Rabbit. "Very glad to help."

"Good-by, now," said the little girl.

"Good-by," said Mr. Rabbit, "and a happy birthday and a happy basket of fruit to your mother."

Self-Assessment

Encourage children to think about their reading by asking themselves:

- How do my predictions match what happened in the story?

- What clues did I use to decide what would happen next?

QuickREFERENCE

 Multicultural Link

Ask children who know languages other than English how to say "Happy Birthday" in those languages. You might get them started by saying "Happy Birthday" in Spanish:

Feliz cumpleaños

 Extra Support

Remind children that when the girl thanked Mr. Rabbit, he said, "Not at all." Ask what Mr. Rabbit meant. Elicit that *not at all* means much the same thing as "you're welcome." It's a short way of saying "It was no trouble at all."

Concept Development

Color

Teach/ Model

Display the picture on page 29 as you read aloud the last paragraph on page 28. Then ask children to point to the green pears, the yellow bananas, the red apples, and the blue grapes in the picture.

Print the color words on the board:

> green
> yellow
> red
> blue

Read aloud the first word. Ask children to draw pictures of other foods that are green. (You may want to brainstorm a list of such foods with children.)

Repeat for the remaining colors. Then challenge children to name other colors, as well as foods that are those colors.

Practice/Apply

Invite children to find and clip from old magazines as many color pictures of food as they can. Have children sort the foods according to color. They may want to add some of the pictures to the *Color Is Everywhere* bulletin board.

SKILL FINDER

Minilessons: pp. T135, T159

2

Interact with Literature

Rereading

Choices for Rereading

Reading for Details

To promote story comprehension, pause after reading the following pages and ask these questions:

- Page 6: Why did the little girl need Mr. Rabbit's help? (She needed a present for her mother's birthday.)

- Page 10: Why didn't the girl want to give her mother a red roof or a red bird? (Her family had a roof; her mother liked birds in trees.)

- Page 12: Did the little girl think that red apples were enough of a present? (no) How do you know? (She said she needed something else.)

- Page 16: Why couldn't the little girl give her mother the yellow sun? (You can't take the sun from the sky and give it to someone.)

- Page 20: Why couldn't the little girl give her mother green emeralds? (They cost a lot of money; the girl didn't have money.)

- Page 28: What did the little girl give her mother? (red apples, yellow bananas, green pears, blue grapes—in a basket)

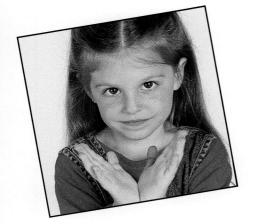

Creating Titles

Reread *Mr. Rabbit and the Lovely Present* in the following sections. Help children think of a title for each one. (Possible titles are shown in parentheses.)

- Pages 4-7 ("A Present")

- Pages 8-13 ("Something Red")

- Pages 14-19 ("Something Yellow")

- Pages 20-23 ("Something Green")

- Pages 24-27 ("Something Blue")

- Pages 28-31 ("A Basket of Fruit")

Story Language Pattern

As you reread *Mr. Rabbit and the Lovely Present,* pause occasionally after one of Mr. Rabbit's lines. Ask children how they think the little girl responds. For example, after Mr. Rabbit says "There are red roofs," children could be familiar enough with the story to suggest that her family already has a roof. After he says "There are apples," children could recall that red apples are a good idea.

Informal Assessment

Use the activities on this page, especially Reading for Details, to assess children's understanding of the story. Also note with each rereading whether they understand that print is read from left to right.

Responding

Choices for Responding

Using Story Retelling Props

Invite children to use the Story Retelling Props to retell *Mr. Rabbit and the Lovely Present.* Lay the poster on a flat surface and put the story pieces in the appropriate places. Ask pairs of children to take turns using the puppets to role play the little girl and Mr. Rabbit. As the child playing Mr. Rabbit suggests different gifts from the poster, the child playing the little girl can take the fruits and place them in the basket. Encourage children to invent dialogue for the characters.

Students Acquiring English Retelling with props is very helpful for children acquiring English because the props help make the oral language more comprehensible.

> **Materials**
>
> Story Retelling Props: story pieces, poster, and puppets for *Mr. Rabbit and the Lovely Present*
>
> (See Teacher's Handbook, page H4.)

 ### Home Connection

Have children make their own retelling props: a tagboard girl, a tagboard rabbit, the fruits, and a basket. Suggest that they retell the story at home and give the basket of fruit to someone as a present.

Students Acquiring English Home links are crucial for students acquiring English. Children can retell the story to family members in their primary language.

Personal Response

Ask children to imagine that they could meet Mr. Rabbit. What would they ask him? What would they tell him? Children might work with partners to role play a meeting with Mr. Rabbit. Partners can take turns playing the part of the rabbit.

Portfolio Opportunity

For an oral sample, tape-record the retelling activity in which children use the Story Retelling Props.

Instruct and Integrate

Comprehension

Literacy Activity Book, p. 16

Materials
- red apple
- another red object

Informal Assessment

As children complete the activities on this page, note their ability to use inferencing skills to make predictions and to identify words that end with the same sounds.

Practice Activities

Inferences: Making Predictions

LAB, p. 16

Extra Support Hold up a red apple, together with something else (other than another fruit) that is red. Ask which red thing the little girl in the story chose for her mother's birthday basket. If necessary, reread page 12 of the story as you display the picture on page 13.

Discuss how the little girl used her mother's favorite colors and fruits to put together a lovely birthday present.

Next, display the picture on page 31 of the story. Ask children if they think the little girl's mother will like the basket of fruit. Encourage them to give reasons for their answers. Elicit that since the girl has chosen her mother's favorite colors and fruits, it is very likely that her mother will be very pleased.

Ask children to predict what the girl's mother will do with the basket of fruit. What would they do if they were the girl's mother?

Have children complete *Literacy Activity Book,* page 16.

The Birthday Party

Have small groups of children dictate a story about what might happen next in the story *Mr. Rabbit and the Lovely Present.* Share all of the sequels and allow time for children to comment on them.

Students Acquiring English Placing children acquiring English in mixed language groupings for this activity will help them gain proficiency.

Whose Picnic Is This?

Display the picture on page 19 of *Mr. Rabbit and the Lovely Present.* Have children speculate about the picnic scene. Who was picnicking there? Did the picnickers come back? Invite children to draw pictures to show what they think.

Phonemic Awareness

Practice Activities

Rhyme Time

LAB, p. 17

Extra Support Ask children to listen as you reread the Theme Poem "What Is Pink?" Then tell them that you will say three words from the poem. They are to listen carefully and then repeat the two words that rhyme. Say these words, repeating each set several times, if necessary:

- bed, rose, red
- pink, brink, blue
- sky, blue, through
- white, swan, light
- green, pear, between

Then have children complete *Literacy Activity Book,* page 17. For further support, you might also have groups of two to four children play the game Color Round the Rhyme.

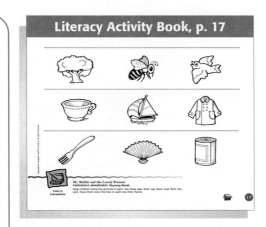

Literacy Activity Book, p. 17

Materials

- Audio Tape: Color Is Everywhere: "What Is Pink?"
- *LAB,* p. 17
- Game: Color Round the Rhyme (See Teacher's Handbook, page H8.)

A World of Colors

Print this poem (author unknown) on chart paper and save for re-use later.

Read the poem aloud. Ask children to listen for two words that rhyme. *(green, between)*

Then have children listen as you say *clean, pink, seen, bean,* and *ten* one at a time, and raise their hands if a word rhymes with *green* and *between.*

I'm Glad the Sky Is Painted Blue

I'm glad the sky is painted blue,
And the earth is painted green,
With such a lot of nice fresh air
All sandwiched in between.

Nursery Rhymes

Read aloud the following nursery rhyme. After an initial reading, ask children to listen again for rhyming words.

Twinkle, twinkle, little star,

How I wonder what you are!

Up above the world so high,

Like a diamond in the sky.

Challenge Children might cut out star shapes and write two rhyming words on each star, one to a side.

Portfolio Opportunity

Save *Literacy Activity Book,* page 17, as a record of children's ability to recognize rhyming words. You might also include children's picnic pictures to show their ability to make predictions.

Instruct *and* **Integrate**

Oral Language

Poster

Informal Assessment

As children give their talks about perfect presents, note whether or not they include information for each bulleted item. Also make note of children's contributions to writing activities.

Choices for Oral Language

What's the Present?

- Find a box large enough for a child to fit a hand in.

- Cut a hole in the top of the box and then gift wrap it to make it look like a lovely present.

- Choose a familiar object and place it in the box.

- Pass the box around the class, allowing children to feel what's inside. Ask children to describe the object and to try to guess what it is.

- Continue the activity, using other objects.

Perfect Presents

Invite children to tell about presents they have made for friends or family members. Encourage each child to make a short "talk" in which he or she tells:

- Who the present was for

- What the occasion was

- How the present was made

- How the person receiving the gift seemed to feel about it

A Basket of Vegetables

Display the Market Colors poster and identify the fruits and vegetables. Ask children to imagine that the little girl decided to give her mother a basket of vegetables instead of fruits. Work with children to brainstorm a list of vegetables.

Invite children to draw a picture of a basket of vegetables. Have them share their pictures, naming the vegetables they've chosen.

The Colors of Birds

Display several pictures of birds of different colors. (Use pictures children have found, if you've done the science activity suggested on page T111.) Name the different birds for children and then ask children to describe their coloration. Ask children who may have seen such birds in their yards to tell about them.

You might add pictures of some of the birds to the *Color Is Everywhere* bulletin board.

Writing

Our Fruit Salad Recipe

Help children recall the fruits mentioned in *Mr. Rabbit and the Lovely Present.* Then discuss how the girl's mother might use her present. Might she use it to make a fruit salad?

Invite children to help you make a fruit salad for the class. Provide several fruits. Encourage children to name each fruit and to describe the steps you take to make the salad, such as washing the fruit, coring the apples, and mixing all the fruit together. List the steps on chart paper in recipe form, then read the recipe aloud to children. Encourage them to join in as you read.

Children might make their own copies of the recipe to take home as a present.

A Card Can Be a Present

Point out to children that homemade cards make lovely presents. Encourage each child to make a card for a friend or family member. Children can write or dictate messages for their cards.

If some children wish to make birthday cards, print *Happy Birthday* on a sheet of folded construction paper. Place your greeting on a table, along with folded cards for children to use.

Every Day Is a Gift

Display the poem "I'm Glad the Sky Is Painted Blue." (See page T121.) Note that depending on the weather and the time of year, the sky can be different colors and so can the earth. Talk about the sky on a rainy day and the earth on a snowy day. Then invite children to draw pictures of their favorite way to see the sky and the earth. They can then write or dictate a few words about their pictures.

Tell children every day is a special gift--a chance to see and do new things. Encourage children to give their pictures away as gifts.

Portfolio Opportunity

If children don't give away their cards or sky and earth pictures, save them as a record of their writing.

Cross-Curricular Activities

Science

Materials
- several kinds of fruits
- pots
- potting soil

Which Came First?

Challenge Explain that inside most fruits are seeds. These seeds are the "starts" of new plants. The new plants will eventually produce fruits just like the ones from which the seeds came. Invite children to explore the different kinds of seeds found in common fruits.

- Cut the fruits in half.

- Remove the seeds and examine them with children. Which fruits have big seeds, or pits? Which have little seeds? Are there "sprouts" showing on any of the seeds?

- Provide pots and potting soil. Help children plant a few seeds and label the pots.

- Assign plant waterers and watch to see if plants grow.

Choices for Math

A Birthday Calendar

Each month highlight children's birthdays on a page-a-month calendar. At some time during the year, have an "unbirthday" party for children whose birthdays occur during vacation or whenever school is not in session.

Favorite Color Graph

Make a graph with children's names down the left and the color names *red, orange, yellow, green, blue, purple* across the top. Show children how to fill in the square that represents their favorite color. When the graph is complete, have children help to figure out the results.

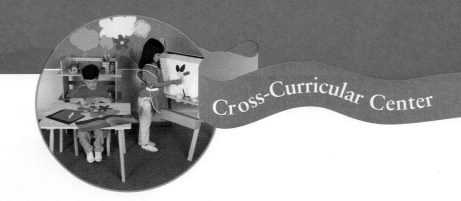
Art

Play Dough Fruits

Talk with children about the shapes of several different familiar fruits. Then have each child choose a fruit to make from the play dough. If necessary, demonstrate how to shape the dough into a ball or a cylinder. Little sticks can be used for stems. When the fruits are dry, they can be painted. (Craft glue can be used to hold grapes in bunches.) Display children's creations in the "Art Gallery."

Play Dough Recipe

1 1/2 cups corn starch

1/2 cup flour

2 teaspoons cream of tartar

2 cups water

1 tablespoon vegetable oil

Mix in saucepan. Cook over medium heat, stirring constantly for about 5 minutes, until the mixture gets sticky and forms dough. Cool a bit on a plate. Then knead the mixture to make it smooth. Keep in covered container until it's time to use it.

Science

Now Do You Like Me?

Recall with children that the little girl's mother did not like green caterpillars. Explain that some green caterpillars turn into pretty butterflies. Have children share what they know about butterflies. If possible, have pictures available of caterpillars and butterflies. Then provide paper and crayons for children to make caterpillars and butterflies to decorate the classroom.

BIG BOOK

SELECTION:

Rain

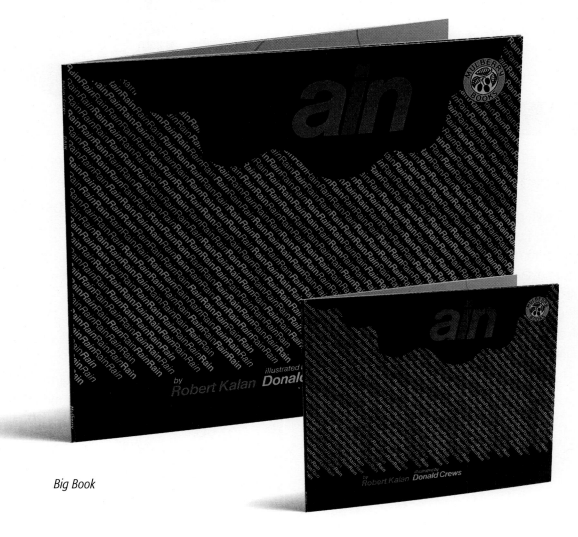

Big Book

Little Big Book

● **Best Books for Children**

by Robert Kalan

Other Books by Robert Kalan

Blue Sea

Stop, Thief!

Selection Summary

A sunny, blue-sky day turns gray and cloudy. Then the rain comes down—on the black road, on the red car, on the orange flowers. But when the rain finally stops, a beautiful rainbow fills the sky.

Lesson Planning Guide

	Skill/Strategy Instruction	Meeting Individual Needs	Lesson Resources
1 Introduce *the* Literature *Pacing: 1 day*	**Shared Reading and Writing** Warm-Up/Build Background, T128 Shared Reading, T128 Shared Writing, T129	Choices for Rereading, T129	**Poster** Rain Song, T128 *Literacy Activity Book* Personal Response, p. 18
2 Interact *with* Literature *Pacing: 1–2 days*	**Reading Strategies** Self-Question, T130, T132 Monitor, T130, T132 Evaluate, T132, T136 Think About Words, T138 **Minilessons** ✔ Story Structure (Beginning), T131 Story Structure (Middle), T133 Color, T135 ✔ Directionality, T137 Story Structure (End), T139	**Students Acquiring English,** T131, T136, T139, T141 **Challenge,** T135, T138 **Extra Support,** T137, T140 **Rereading and Responding,** T140–T141	**Story Props,** T141, H5 *Literacy Activity Book* Language Patterns, p. 19 See the Houghton Mifflin **Internet** resources for additional activities.
3 Instruct *and* Integrate *Pacing: 1–2 days*	**Reading/Listening Center** Comprehension, T142 Concept Development, T143 Concepts About Print, T144 Listening, T145 **Language/Writing Center** Oral Language, T146 Writing, T147 **Cross-Curricular Center** Cross-Curricular Activities, T148–T149	**Extra Support,** T142, T144 **Challenge,** T144, T147, T148 **Students Acquiring English,** T146	*Literacy Activity Book* Comprehension, p. 20 Concept Development, p. 21 **Audio Tape** for Color Is Everywhere: *Rain* See the Houghton Mifflin **Internet** resources for additional activities.

✔ *Indicates Tested Skills. See page T103 for assessment options.*

1 Introduce *the* Literature

Shared Reading and Writing

INTERACTIVE LEARNING

Poster

Literacy Activity Book, p. 18

Warm-Up/Build Background

Sharing a Poem

- Ask children to close their eyes and try to picture rain in their minds. What colors do they see when they think about rain?

- Display the poster for "Rain Song" and read aloud the title of the poem. Discuss the illustration with children. Did they picture any of these same colors when they tried to think about rain?

- Read "Rain Song" for children. Explain that the poem tells about rain in each of the four seasons: spring, summer, fall, winter. Ask why someone might think of a spring rain as being pink or a fall rain as being brown. (Depending on where you live and children's backgrounds, you may need to talk about seasonal changes or show pictures of such changes.)

- Read the poem again. Ask children to close their eyes once more and try to picture the colors of rain as they listen.

- Point to the word *Rain* in the title of the poem and ask children to help you name the letters in the word. *(R-a-i-n)*

Shared Reading

LAB, p. 18

Preview and Predict

- Display *Rain* and point to the book's title. Invite children to read the title along with you. Then discuss how Donald Crews, who illustrated this book, used the letters *R-a-i-n* to make a picture of falling rain.

- Ask children what they think this book is about. If necessary, explain that readers can often tell what a book is about from its title.

Read Together

- Read the book for children. Pause occasionally to ask them to match pictures with text. You might, for example, ask volunteers to point to the *yellow* sun, the *white* clouds, and the *gray* sky in the pictures.

- Discuss the story's ending with children. Ask if they have ever seen a rainbow after a rainstorm. What did the rainbow look like?

Personal Response

Ask if children like to be outdoors when it rains. Encourage them to tell how the rain looks and feels. Then have children complete *Literacy Activity Book,* page 18.

Shared Writing: *A Class Story*

Brainstorming
Invite children to help you write a class story about rain. Ask several volunteers to tell what they like to do on rainy days. Do they play indoors? Do they listen for the sound of rain on the windowpanes? Do they go outdoors and splash through puddles?

Ask each child to draw a picture to show what he or she likes to do most when it rains. As children are drawing, write the title *When It Rains* at the top of a piece of chart paper.

Drafting
Invite children to take turns sharing their pictures. The child whose turn it is should dictate a sentence that tells what he or she likes to do when it rains. Write each child's sentence on the chart, followed by the child's name. If children have difficulty, use a sentence frame such as this:

> **When it rains, I like to _____.**

Publishing
Have children write their names on their pictures. Then display the class story, together with children's pictures, on a bulletin board. Reread the story for children. Invite children to help read those sentences they've contributed.

Choices for Rereading

Rereadings provide varied, repeated experiences with the literature so that children can make its language and content their own. The following rereading choices appear on page T140.

- Recognizing Language Patterns
- Adding Sound Effects: It's Raining!
- Cooperative Reading

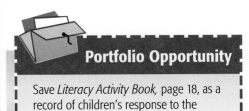

Portfolio Opportunity

Save *Literacy Activity Book,* page 18, as a record of children's response to the literature.

BIG BOOK

Reading Strategies

▶ **Self-Question**
Monitor

Discussion Remind children that good readers *think* as they read. They ask themselves what questions a book might answer. They also ask themselves if what they are reading makes sense.

Help children recall that the title of this book is *Rain.* Ask what questions a book with this title might answer. Elicit several responses.

Reread pages 5–7 with children. Ask if they wondered about the title the first time they read this book. Do these pages tell about rain? Review that if what we read seems confusing at first, we can read on to see if things become clearer.

Purpose Setting

Invite children to read the story with you to see if their questions are answered and if reading on helps them understand why this book is called *Rain.*

Yellow Sun

6

QuickREFERENCE

Visual Literacy

Children may wonder about the absence of any object on page 5. Explain that the artist, Donald Crews, wanted to show how blue the sky was by having nothing but blue on the page. Ask if children like this way of showing blue sky.

Science Link

Ask if children have ever seen clouds like the ones in the picture on page 7. Explain that fluffy white clouds are often seen in the sky on a nice day. Ask children to look out the window and see if there are any clouds.

Visual Literacy

Help children note that the words of this story are printed in the same colors as the objects they tell about. The words *Yellow sun* are printed in yellow; the words *White clouds* are printed in white.

Blue Sky

5

White clouds

7

Students Acquiring English

Help children understand that in English adjectives most often precede the noun. *(Yellow Sun)* In many other languages the adjective follows the noun. *(French–le soleil jaune) (Spanish–el sol amarillo)*

Comprehension

Story Structure (Beginning)

TESTED SKILL

Teach/Model

Be sure children understand the words *beginning, middle,* and *end.* Ask three children to come to the front of the room. Line them up by size. Ask who is standing at the beginning of the line. In the middle? At the end?

Think Aloud

I know that a story has a beginning, a middle, and an end. The beginning is how the story starts. It's the first part of the story.

Read pages 5–7. Then ask children to tell how this story begins. What kind of day is it?

Practice/Apply

Ask children to tell how their day began. What was the first thing they did? What was the weather like outside?

Ask each child to draw a picture to show something he or she did at the very beginning of this day. Children might include windows to show what the weather outside was like. (Save children's pictures.)

SKILL FINDER

Story Mural, p. T142

Minilessons: Themes 10, 12

Interact
with
Literature

Reading Strategies

▶ **Self-Question**
Evaluate

Discussion Discuss how the weather changes in this part of the story. Ask if children were surprised that the sky turned gray and that it began to rain. Talk about whether reading on helped answer why the story is called *Rain* or any other questions they may have asked themselves.

Have children compare the picture on page 11 with the cover of *Rain*. Ask what the artist used—instead of raindrops—to show falling rain. (the word *Rain*, repeated again and again, falling from the clouds) Encourage children to discuss whether or not they like how the artist uses the word to represent raindrops and why.

Gray clouds

8

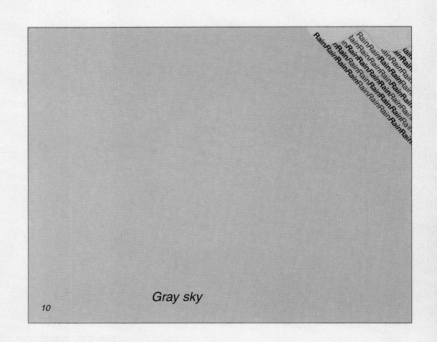

Gray sky

10

QuickREFERENCE

Visual Literacy

Ask children what they think has happened to the sun in the picture on page 9. (It's behind the clouds; it can't be seen now.) You may also want to point out that the clouds are different shades of gray; some are darker gray than others.

Media Link

If you have access to TV, invite children to view a weather report with you. Have them listen for information about sky color and clouds.

 ### Journal

Invite children to draw pictures of rain using the letters in the word. Then have them write or dictate a few words telling how they feel when it rains outside.

No sun

9

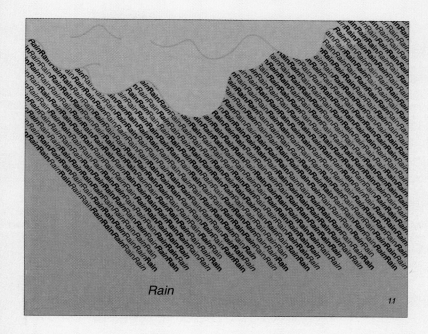

Rain

11

Comprehension
Story Structure (Middle)

Teach/Model

Place two books on a table, leaving a space between them. Ask a volunteer to put another book in the middle. Then ask another child to point to the *middle* book. Be sure children understand that if something is in the middle, it is between two things.

Think Aloud

I know that a story has a middle. The middle of a story is the part between the beginning and the end. The middle of a story is often a much longer part than the beginning or the end. The middle part of *Rain* begins here. (Show page 8.) The middle part tells about the rain, and it goes all the way to this page. (Leaf through to page 21.)

Practice/Apply

Ask children to draw pictures that show something they do in the middle of the day. Compare these with the pictures children drew to show the day's beginning.

SKILL FINDER

Story Mural, p. T142

Minilessons: Themes 10, 12

Science Link

Explain to children that a cloud is a collection of many water droplets or ice particles in the air.

Interact
with
Literature

Rain on the green grass

12

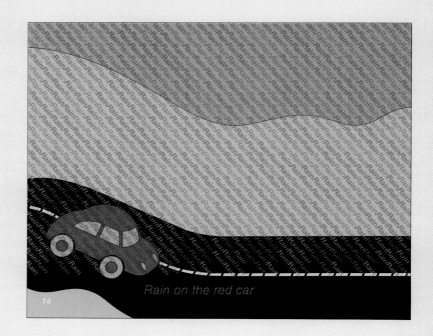

Rain on the red car

14

Big Book pp. 12, 14

QuickREFERENCE

Visual Literacy

Direct children's attention to page 12. Ask them what color is used for the words *Rain on the green grass*. (green) Point out the green area that spreads across pages 12–13. Explain that this light green color is the grass.

Social Studies Link

Have children run their fingers along the road in the picture on page 13. Ask how people use roads. Point out the picture of the car on page 14. Ask what else travels along roads besides cars carrying people. (trucks carrying things to market, buses)

Science Link

Use the picture on pages 14–15 to explore with children why we need rain. Elicit that rain helps flowers and plants grow. Point out that rain also provides people and animals with drinking water.

Rain on the black road

13

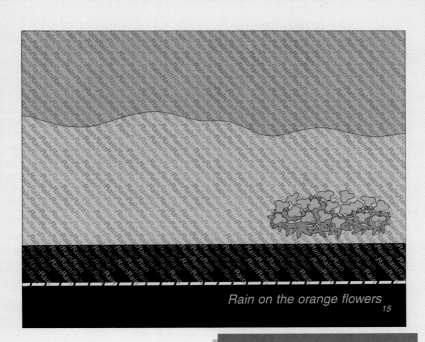

Rain on the orange flowers

15

MEETING INDIVIDUAL NEEDS

Challenge

Point out that the people in the car on page 14 won't get wet. Ask children what they would use to avoid getting wet if they weren't in a car.
(raincoat, umbrella, hat, rain shoes)

Concept Development
Color

Teach/Model

Help children make a color chart for the colors mentioned thus far in the story. List each color name in one column; then hold up a crayon of that color and ask children to color with it in the second column.

blue	
yellow	
white	
gray	
green	
black	
red	
orange	

Have children find each color name in the story and then name the object that is that color.

Practice/Apply

Ask each child to choose one color crayon, write the color name at the top of a piece of paper, and then draw pictures of several objects that are this color. Display children's pictures on a bulletin board.

SKILL FINDER

All the Colors of the Rainbow, p. T143

Minilessons, pages T117, T159

Interact *with* Literature

BIG BOOK

Reading Strategies

▶ **Evaluate**

Ask children how they feel about this story. Use these prompts:

- Did you like the story? Why or why not?

- Did you like the way colors were used for the words of the story?

- Did you like the way Donald Crews used the word *Rain* to make the rainfall in his pictures?

Rain on the brown fence

18   Rain on the white house

QuickREFERENCE

Visual Literacy

Ask children to find the brown fence and the purple flowers in the picture on pages 16–17. Then ask them to find these same things in the picture on pages 18–19.

 Students Acquiring English

The Evaluate reading strategy will help children acquiring English get meaning out of the story. Allow them to discuss the questions in mixed or same language groupings.

Rain on the purple flowers

17

Rain on the green trees

19

Extra Support

Explain to children that fences have many uses. Fences can be used to keep things out, to keep things in, to mark boundaries, or for decoration. Help children brainstorm a list of places where they have seen fences.

Concepts About Print
Directionality

Teach/Model

Point out the position of the red car on pages 16–17. Run your hand from left to right across the page to show the direction in which the car is "moving" along the road.

Think Aloud

I know that the car in this story is moving from left to right. This is the same direction that I'm supposed to read the words on a page—from left to right. Watch as I read the words on this page. (Reread page 16, running your hand under the words from left to right.) I'm reading in the same direction that the car is going.

Repeat with the words on page 17.

Note: If children are confused by all the small words in the rain, explain that these are part of the art; they are not meant to be read.

Practice/Apply

Turn to pages 18–19. Ask a child to show which page to read first. (left page) Ask other children to show the direction in which the words on each page should be read.

SKILL FINDER

Directional Rules, p. T144

Minilessons: Themes 6, 7

Interact *with* Literature

Reading Strategies

 Think About Words

Ask children how they could figure out the meaning of *rainbow* on page 22 if they didn't know the word.

What makes sense I hear the words *rain* and *bow* in *rainbow*. I know what rain is, and I know one kind of *bow* is a shape like a half circle.

Picture clues In the picture, I see a half circle made up of lots of colors. I think this must be a rainbow.

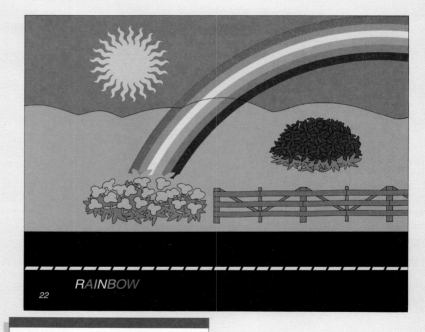

Self-Assessment

Have children ask themselves:

● If I don't know what a word means, what do I do? Do I think about what makes sense? Do I look at pictures? Do I ask for help?

● Can I find the beginning, middle, and end of a story?

Quick**REFERENCE**

 ★★★ **Multicultural Link**

Invite children who speak languages other than English to share their words for *rainbow*. For example:
● *el arco iris* (Spanish)
● *l'arc-en-ciel* (French)

 Challenge

Ask children why pages 20–21 are so dark. Help children understand that when it rains heavily the sky becomes very dark, even during the day.

Visual Literacy/Print Awareness

Point out that the word *rainbow* is written in all capital letters on page 22. It is also written in all the colors of the rainbow! Have children name each letter and its color as you point to the letters from left to right.

Rain

21

Comprehension

Story Structure (End)

Teach/Model

Ask a child to point to the *end* of something, such as an alphabet chart. Ask what they might do at the end of a movie or TV program. (clap; turn the TV off)

Think Aloud

I know that the end of a story is the very last thing that happens. It's usually the last page or two of a book. Watch as I hold up the pages at the end of *Rain*. (Display pages 22–23.) What happens at the very end of this story about rain? (The sun comes out and a rainbow appears in the sky.)

Practice/Apply

Ask children to draw pictures that show what they do at the very end of the day. Compare these with the pictures children drew to show the day's beginning and middle. Then have children display their pictures in order, from beginning to end.

SKILL FINDER

Story Mural, p. T142

Minilessons: Themes 10, 12

Science Link

Explain that rainbows are caused by sunlight shining through water in the air. You might hang a prism in a classroom window where it will catch the sunlight and cast a rainbow on the walls. Ask children to name the colors they see.

MEETING INDIVIDUAL NEEDS

Students Acquiring English

Have children discuss how many color words they have in their language. Since cultures divide the color spectrum differently, children may not see the colors and shades exactly alike.

Rereading

Literacy Activity Book, p. 19

Rain

Choices for Rereading

Recognizing Language Patterns

LAB, p. 19

Reread *Rain* with children. Help them note the repeating language pattern:

Rain on the (color word) (name of object)

Brainstorm a list of things rain might fall on—besides those mentioned in the book. For example:

bus   **school**

sidewalk

Ask children to think of a color for each thing. Write the color word before the name of the object. Then ask children to use the words to finish the phrase:

Rain on the _____

Provide practice with story language patterns by having children complete *Literacy Activity Book,* page 19.

Materials

Felt or paper color samples: blue, yellow, white, gray, green, black, red, orange, brown, purple

Informal Assessment

- Use the activities on this page to assess children's general understanding of the selection.
- Note whether children comprehend that print is read from left to right.

Cooperative Reading

Give each child one color sample. As you reread *Rain,* invite children with the color for that page to read along with you. If necessary, cue children by saying something like "It's your turn, blue" at the appropriate places in the story.

Extra Support Children might echo read the text instead of reading it along with you.

Adding Sound Effects: It's Raining!

Choose a small group of children to read the text of *Rain* along with you. Other children should tap their fingers on a table or desktop to represent rain. They should begin and end their tapping at appropriate times in the story; they should tap gently or hard to show *how* the rain is falling.

Responding

Choices for Responding

Retelling the Story

Invite children to use the Story Retelling Props to retell the beginning, the middle, and the end of *Rain.* Be sure children understand how to move the toy car from left to right across the mat or mural they have created.

Children might work in groups of three for the retelling, with one child responsible for each part. Children can then change roles so that everyone has the opportunity to retell the longer middle part.

Students Acquiring English Invite children with limited English proficiency to retell the story in same language groups.

> **Materials**
> Story Retelling
> Props: Teacher's
> Handbook, page H5

🏠 Personal Response

Ask children to tell what the weather is like right now. Is it raining? Is the sun shining? Have each child draw a picture of the rain (or the sun or the snow) or something they can see from the classroom window.

On the other side of their papers, children can draw a favorite scene from the story *Rain.* If they choose a rain scene, they might write the word *Rain* many times to represent rain, just as Donald Crews did.

Children can take their drawings home to share the story as well as their own weather pictures with family members.

Making Rainbows

Display pages 22–23 of *Rain* and have children name the colors that make up this rainbow. Invite children to make their own rainbows.

1. Have children spread newspaper as you mix the dishwashing detergent with water.

2. Show children how to dip their wands into the solution and then gently blow to create bubbles.

3. Have children look for colors of the rainbow in their bubbles.

> **Materials**
> • wire wands
> • dishwashing detergent

3

Instruct *and* Integrate

Comprehension

Literacy Activity Book, p. 20

Practice Activities

Story Mural

LAB, p. 20

Extra Support Divide the mural paper into three sections, with the middle section substantially larger than the other two. Using self-stick notes (which can later be removed) label the sections *beginning, middle, end.*

Materials
- mural paper
- paints
- self-stick notes

Invite children to paint a mural showing the beginning, middle, and end of *Rain.* Point to these parts on the mural paper. Discuss with children what they will show in each section, referring to the Big Book as necessary.

Have children use their completed mural to tell

- what the weather was like at the beginning of the story (sunny)
- what it was like in the middle of the story (rainy)
- what appeared in the sky at the end of the story (a rainbow)

Have children complete *Literacy Activity Book,* page 20.

Materials
- Felt or paper color samples: blue, yellow, white, gray, green, black, red, orange, brown, purple

Categorizing Colors

Give each child a set of color samples. Talk about different ways the colors might be sorted. For example:

- Colors I like/Colors I don't like
- Colors I'm wearing/Colors I'm not wearing
- Bright colors/Dull colors
- Dark colors/Light colors

Have each child choose a category and then sort the colors accordingly.

Beginning, Middle, End

Reread *Mr. Rabbit and the Lovely Present* to children. Then help them identify the beginning, the middle, and the end of this story.

- Beginning—The little girl asks Mr. Rabbit for help choosing a birthday present for her mother.
- Middle—Mr. Rabbit helps the girl choose red apples, yellow bananas, green pears, and blue grapes.
- End—The girl thanks Mr. Rabbit for his help.

Informal Assessment

Note children's ability to identify the beginning, the middle, and the end of a story. Also observe their ability to identify and categorize colors.

Concept Development

Practice Activities

Weather

Help children make a weather chart and record the kind of weather that occurs each day for a week. For example:

Monday	Tuesday	Wednesday	Thursday	Friday
sunny	cloudy	rainy	sunny	sunny

All the Colors of the Rainbow

LAB, p. 21

Display pages 22–23 of *Rain.* Then name one of the rainbow colors, such as *red*, and ask volunteers to find pictures of things in *Rain* that are that color. Repeat for the remaining colors.

Ask children to look out the window to find something else that is red, orange, yellow, green, blue, or purple. Then distribute crayons for these colors, and have children complete *Literacy Activity Book,* page 21.

Home Connection Invite children to take *Literacy Activity Book* page 21 home to share their observations with family members.

How to Make a Gray Cloud

Ask a child to paint a white cloud on a sheet of blue paper. Then, in a small container, mix white paint with a little black as children observe. Ask them to name the color you made. (gray)

Ask what children think will happen if you add more black to the gray. Do so as children watch. Were their predictions correct?

Invite children to mix paint to make different shades of gray. Children can then paint pictures of clouds.

Literacy Activity Book, p. 21

[Literacy Activity Book page showing: yellow sun, green tree, black road, red car]

Rain
CONCEPT DEVELOPMENT Color Words
Color is Everywhere

Dear Family,
On your next walk together, take along paper and colored markers or crayons. Take turns drawing and coloring pictures of things you see. When you get home, write the color words on each picture at your child tells you its color.

Materials
- light blue construction paper
- white and black paint
- brushes
- small cups for mixing paint

Portfolio Opportunity

Save *Literacy Activity Book,* page 20, as a record of children's understanding of story structure.

Instruct *and* Integrate

Concepts About Print

Practice Activities

Directional Rules

Extra Support Display the Big Book *ABC and You* from the previous theme. Ask what children recall about this book. If necessary, remind them that the letters of the alphabet appear in order, and that for each letter, there are words telling about a child whose name begins with that letter.

Remind children that when they read, they read the print from left to right and from the top to the bottom of the page. Open to the first page of the book and ask a volunteer to tell where you should begin to read.

Reread the book with children, calling on volunteers to help you by using their hands in a sweeping motion across the page from left to right. As you are about to begin reading each page, have a volunteer point to the place where the class should begin reading.

Scratchboard Art

Invite children to make scratchboard nameplates. They can use favorite colors (except black) to completely color a piece of cardboard. Then they should use a black crayon to completely cover the cardboard again.

Show children how to scrape away the black crayon to write their names. Invite them to count the number of letters in their name.

Children can use their nameplates to identify their desks or cubbies.

Rainbow Letters

Remind children that in the last theme they learned about the letters of the alphabet. Invite children to use rainbow-colored paints to make letters that they know.

Challenge Children might also enjoy writing in rainbow colors the names of friends or family members, and then counting the number of letters in each of the names.

Materials
- red, orange, yellow, green, blue, and purple paint
- brushes

Materials
- cardboard
- crayons of different colors, including black

Informal Assessment

As children complete the activities, note their use of directional rules, knowledge of letter concepts, and their ability to listen.

Listening

Practice Activities

Listen and Read!

 Audio Tape for Color is Everywhere: *Rain*

Place copies of the Little Big Book *Rain,* along with the Audio Tape, in the Reading/Listening Center. As children listen to the tape, they can run their hands under the words, from left to right, to show their understanding of concepts about print (directional rules).

A Story from YOU!

Invite children to listen as you tell them a story about rain, based on your own experiences. You might want to use these questions to help shape your story:

- Where did you live when you were in kindergarten?

- What was the weather like there? Was there too much rain? Not enough rain?

- What did you wear when you went out in the rain? Did you have your own umbrella? Did you like to splash in rain puddles?

I Spy

Invite children to play "I Spy." One child should choose a single-colored object in the classroom, for example, a red apple. The children should then give a color clue for the object, using the following sentence:

> **I spy with my little eye something *red*.**

Whoever names the correct answer can choose the next object and continue the game.

Japanese Rain Song

★★★ Print "Japanese Rain Song" on the board or on chart paper. Ask children to listen as you recite the words. Then invite children to recite the song along with you.

Japanese Rain Song

Pitter-patter, falling, falling,

rain is falling down.

Mother comes to bring umbrella,

rain is falling down.

Pi chi, pi chi, cha pu, cha pu,

rain, rain, rain.

Instruct and Integrate

Oral Language

Choices for Oral Language

A Play About Rain

Help children plan a dramatization of the book *Rain.*

- Assign each page to one or more children to memorize and to illustrate in their own way.

- Have children decide whether to place their "scenery" on the "stage" in some way (for such lines as "Rain on the orange flowers") or to carry it with them (for such lines as "White clouds").

- For the performance, help children line up in the order of their lines from the story. Then, one at a time, they can be "on stage," act out their lines, and move off to the other side.

- You might video tape the play so children can watch their own performances. Or, invite another class to come and see it.

Materials
- boots
- rain hats
- raincoats

Dramatic Play

Students Acquiring English Place rainy-day attire in the dramatic play area. Then invite children to dramatize situations (or propose solutions to problems) that may occur on rainy days. For example:

- You and two or three friends are waiting at the corner for the school bus. Suddenly it starts to rain.

- You and your family are on a picnic. You hear thunder in the distance. What will you do?

Weather Words

Display a chart like the one below.

sunny day	rainy day
sunny	rainy
fair	misty

Ask children to help you think of other words to describe a sunny day. List them in the first column. Then ask for words that describe a rainy day. List them in the second column. (Children may suggest such words as *clear, bright, pleasant* and *foggy, dreary, gray.*)

Informal Assessment

As children participate in the oral language and writing activities, make note of their ability to use story language, use temporary spellings, and convey meaning through their drawings.

 # Writing

Choices for Writing

Write a Poem

Invite children to help you write a poem with the title "Red Is." Print the following on the board:

Red Is
Red is an apple
And a _____

Read the first line for children. Then ask a volunteer to think of something else that is red. Print the child's response on the line. Ask if children can think of other things that are red and add these to the poem. As you write, call attention to the fact that you write words from left to right.

Challenge Leave "Red Is" on display and invite children to write their own poems about favorite colors.

Make a Rainbow

Encourage children to draw pictures of rainbows. Invite each child to write or dictate a sentence about his or her picture. You may want to display color charts for children's reference.

Writing About Weather

Have children look through magazines to find pictures of different kinds of weather. Have children cut the pictures out and display them on a bulletin board. Have children work in small groups to choose one picture to write or dictate a caption for. You might demonstrate how to write a caption by choosing one picture and writing an appropriate caption, such as:

> This storm is called a blizzard. A lot of snow falls in a blizzard.

Display children's captions below their pictures.

Materials
- old magazines
- scissors

Portfolio Opportunity

Save children's responses to the writing activities as writing samples.

Instruct
and
Integrate

Cross-Curricular Activities

Science

Water Watch

Materials
- glass, water
- colored marker

Explain that water evaporates into the air from places on the ground and then falls as rain. Fill a glass with water, and draw a line at the water level. The next day, examine the glass with children. Note that the water level has gone down. Draw a line at the water level every day until the water is gone. Ask children where they think the water went. If necessary, remind them that it evaporated, or went into the air.

The Habits of Water

Set up a water table or large tub for children to experiment with water. Encourage children to share their discoveries.

Challenge You might also set up an area for children to experiment with a variety of materials by dipping them in water to see how much they absorb and to see how long they take to dry.

Materials
- water table
- spoons
- measuring cups
- sponge
- magnifying glass

Art

Come See Our Movie

Help children make a stage with rolling scenery from a carton and a roll of paper.

- Place the carton on its side with its opening facing you and cut off the top flaps.

- Cut slits in the back of the carton so that a roll of paper, on which slowly changing weather has been drawn, can be threaded through.

- Place the car at the edge of the stage and slowly pull the paper through. The effect will be that the car—not the scenery—is moving.

- Invite children to retell the story as the scenery moves.

Materials
- cardboard carton
- toy car
- roll paper (fax or shelf paper)
- colored markers

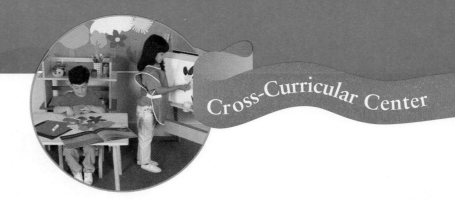

Social Studies

On the Road Again

Display the picture of the road on page 13 of *Rain.* Point out the dashed center line. Explain that drivers must stay to the right of this line, except to pass another vehicle.

Roll out a length of butcher paper and spread it out on the floor. Ask children to "build" their own road or pattern of roads on the paper. (They can use black markers to designate roads; they can glue lengths of yarn down the middle of each road to show center lines)

Have children bring in toy cars and trucks. Children can then move their vehicles around, keeping to the right side of the center line, of course.

Materials
- butcher paper
- black markers
- yellow or white yarn
- toy cars or trucks

Art

Flowers to Rain On

Remind children of the orange and purple flowers in *Rain.* Ask what other colors flowers can be. Provide children with several sheets of colored tissue paper that have been cut into squares. Help children to layer a few squares and then accordion-fold them to form what looks like a fan. Have them fasten the paper at the center with a pipe cleaner and then spread open the tissue layers to create a flower. Children might "plant" their flowers in a class garden on the wall.

Materials
- colored tissue paper
- pipe cleaners

BIG BOOK

SELECTION:
Who Said Red?

Big Book

Little Big Book

by Mary Serfozo

Other Books by Mary Serfozo

Benjamin Bigfoot

Joe Joe

Rain Talk

- **Child Study Children's Book Award**
- **Booklist Editor's Choice**
- **Best Books for Children**
- **Library of Congress Children's Books of the Year**

Selection Summary

"Who said red?" a girl asks her little brother. Despite her attempts to distract him with a variety of colors, the little brother insists that what he wants is red. The reason for his determination becomes clear at the end of the story when readers see the boy's red kite stuck in a bush.

Lesson Planning Guide

	Skill/Strategy Instruction	Meeting Individual Needs	Lesson Resources
1 Introduce *the* Literature *Pacing: 1 day*	**Shared Reading and Writing** Warm-Up/Build Background, T152 Shared Reading, T152 Shared Writing, T153	**Choices for Rereading**, T153	**Poster** Roses Are Red, T152, T179 *Literacy Activity Book* Personal Response, p. 22
2 Interact *with* Literature *Pacing: 1–2 days*	**Reading Strategies** Monitor, T154, T156, T158 Think About Words, T164 Evaluate, T166, T168 **Minilessons** Color, T159 ✓ Directionality/Return Sweep, T161 ✓ Inferences: Drawing Conclusions, T167	**Students Acquiring English**, T154, T158, T162, T165 **Extra Support**, T163, T164 **Challenge**, T157, T160 **Rereading and Responding**, T170–T171	*Literacy Activity Book* Language Patterns, p. 23 See the Houghton Mifflin **Internet** resources for additional activities.
3 Instruct *and* Integrate *Pacing: 1–2 days*	**Reading/Listening Center** Comprehension, T172 Concept Development, T173 Concepts About Print, T174 Listening, T175 **Independent Reading and Writing**, T176–T177 **Language/Writing Center** Oral Language, T178 Writing, T179 **Cross-Curricular Center** Cross-Curricular Activities, T180–T181	**Challenge**, T175, T180 **Extra Support**, T172, T173, T174, T179	*Literacy Activity Book* Comprehension, p. 24 Concept Development, p. 25 Tear-and-Take story, pp. 27–28 **Poster** Signs of Color, T181 **Audio Tape** for Color Is Everywhere: *Who Said Red?* See the Houghton Mifflin **Internet** resources for additional activities.

✓ *Indicates Tested Skills. See page T103 for assessment options.*

1

Introduce *the* Literature

Shared Reading and Writing

Poster

Roses Are Red

Roses are red,
Violets are blue,
Sugar is sweet,
And so are you.

Poster: Color is Everywhere

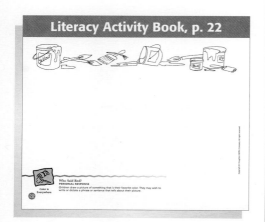

Literacy Activity Book, p. 22

INTERACTIVE LEARNING

Warm-Up/Build Background

Sharing a Poem
- Remind children that in the book *Rain,* the rain fell on orange flowers and purple flowers. Ask if children know the names of any *red* flowers.

- Display the poster for "Roses Are Red," and read the title for children. Have them find the red roses in the picture on the poster. Point out that the blue flowers are called violets.

- Invite children to listen and follow along as you read aloud the rhyme. Then read the rhyme again, encouraging children to join in.

Shared Reading

LAB, p. 22

Preview and Predict
- Display *Who Said Red?* Read aloud the title of the book. Then ask children to point to and name things in the cover illustration that are red.

- Point out that the two characters in this book are a girl and her little brother. Ask children if they can tell from the cover what this book will be about.

- Take a "picture walk" through page 11. Ask if children can tell where this story takes place. (in the country; on a farm) Ask if the pictures on the first few pages give them a better idea of what the story is about.

Read Together
- Read the book for children. Try to use a different voice for each character, so children will understand who is speaking. (The little brother's lines are printed in all capital letters.)

- Pause occasionally to ask if children's predictions match what happens in the story. Invite children to make new predictions.

- Discuss the story's surprise ending with children. Talk about why the boy kept insisting on red. Ask children if there were any clues in the story that the boy wanted his red kite. (Children may recall the red kite in the picture on the cover.)

Personal Response
Ask volunteers to find pages in *Who Said Red?* that show their favorite colors. Then, have children complete *Literacy Activity Book,* page 22.

Shared Writing: *A Class Story*

Brainstorming

Help children compose a sequel to *Who Said Red?* Begin by brainstorming a list of other playthings—and their colors. For example:

stuffed bear–brown	**ball–pink**
toy truck–yellow	**airplane–gray**

As you list children's ideas on the board, you might draw a little picture of each toy they name—to help them recall the items. Have children choose their favorite idea. Then, ask where the little brother in the story might have "lost" that item.

Drafting

Suggest that children begin their stories just like Mary Serfozo did. Print *Who said* (color name)? on the first line of a piece of chart paper. Then invite children to name things—other than the chosen toy— that are that color. Print children's suggestions on the chart. For example:

> **Who said pink?**
>
> A pink rose.
>
> A pink ribbon.

Depending on children's ability, you can help them end the story by having the little brother tell what he really means. Or, you can have children suggest other colors, just as the girl in the story did. Then children can draw pictures to show the ending, that is, where the plaything actually is.

Publishing

Invite children to make illustrations to go with their story. Display their completed story in the Art Gallery.

Choices for Rereading

Rereadings provide varied, repeated experiences with the literature so that children can make its language and content their own. The following rereading choices appear on page T170.

- Recognizing Language Patterns
- Cooperative Reading
- Developing an Ear for Colors

Interact
with
Literature

Reading Strategies

▶ **Monitor**

Student Application Ask children what they can do if they come to a part in a story that they just don't understand right away. Remind them that one thing they can do is to look at the picture for help; another thing to do is to talk over what is confusing with someone else who is reading the story.

Invite children to tell how they could figure out what the author of *Who Said Red?* means when she says "a Santa red." Children should realize that Santa himself is not red. That wouldn't make sense. But his suit and cap are red. They can see this in the picture that shows him riding on the back of the fire engine.

Purpose Setting

Suggest to children that as they read the story with you this time, they think about why the girl keeps naming other colors when her brother keeps on saying *red.*

BIG BOOK

Did you say red?
A Santa red,
A stop sign red,

QuickREFERENCE

Students Acquiring English

Help children understand that it is the girl who is talking on pages 5–7. When she says "you," she is referring to her brother. Invite pairs of children to act out the scene—a girl to say the girl's lines and a boy to listen. When the girl says "you," have her point to the boy.

Who said red?

5

7

Visual Literacy

Have children point, in turn, to the red Santa and the red stop sign. Then have them look for other red things in the picture. (boy's red hair, red socks, red barn, red fire engine, red hats, red part of chickens' heads)

Science Link

Point out the red part of the chickens' heads. Note that this feature, called a comb, makes chickens different from most birds. Explain that some people who know lots about chickens think that the comb helps keep the chickens cool on hot days.

Journal

As children read through the story, encourage them to draw or write about favorite things they own that are the colors mentioned in the story.

Interact *with* Literature

Reading Strategies

▶ **Monitor**

Student Application Ask if children were confused by anything on pages 8–11 of the story. You may want to point out that when the girl says "Look, here is green," she is noticing the green leaves on the trees and the little green frog sitting on a rock. Have children find these things in the pictures on pages 12–15. (You may need to provide help with the tiny frog.)

NOTE:
The overview spreads in this story give hints about what objects will be seen close up on subsequent pages.

QuickREFERENCE

Phonemic Awareness Review

Help children remember that words that end in the same way rhyme. Give the example *cat* and *hat*. Reread page 8 and ask children to listen for three words that rhyme. (cherry, berry, very)

Visual Literacy

Ask children to find something hidden in the picture on page 8. (ladybug) Then see if children can find the little frog almost hidden on page 11.

Science Link

Tell children that the little bug on the strawberry is called a ladybird beetle or a ladybug. These little insects eat even smaller bugs that hurt plants, so farmers like them.

9

You don't mean green?
Look, here is green....

11

Challenge

Model how to read the question and answer on page 10 the way the characters would say them. Then have volunteers try reading the lines dramatically.

Interact *with* Literature

Reading Strategies

▶ **Monitor**

Some children who rely heavily on picture clues and who use those clues literally may be confused by the inclusion of "a tree... green" in the text.

Have children talk about how they made sense of this. They should talk about how they see lots of leaves and that they know that leaves are a part of trees. The picture is showing the leaves that grow on trees and it is the leaves that make up the green part of trees.

A pickle green,
A big frog green,

12

A leaf, a tree,
a green bean green.

14

Quick REFERENCE

Students Acquiring English

Ask children if they like pickles. Pickling is a common way to preserve foods. Have children ask their parents whether (or what) they pickled in their country and why they did it.

13

15

Concept Development
Color

Teach/Model

Recall with children the things the girl mentions that are green. (pickles, frogs, leaves, trees, beans) Say that you would like to add to the list of green things. Make suggestions such as grass and lettuce. Have children agree that each is green. Then invite children to try to add more green things to the list.

Then talk about a color that is only quickly mentioned in the story–brown. Work with children to build a list of brown things. (chocolate, bears, rocks, and so on.)

Practice/Apply

Assign pairs of children a color. They should draw pictures of things that are that color. Have children share their ideas and pictures. Help them label their pictures with the color names.

SKILL FINDER

A World of Colors, page T173

Minilessons: pages T117, T135

Phonemic Awareness Review

Reread page 14 and ask children to listen for two words that end with the same sounds, or rhyme. (*green, bean*)

Visual Literacy/Science Link

See if children can name what they see on the green bean on page 14. If necessary, idenify it as a caterpil-lar. Tell children that caterpillars turn into butterflies. Have them point to the butterfly on page 15.

2 Interact *with* Literature

Did you say green?

NO, I SAID RED!

16

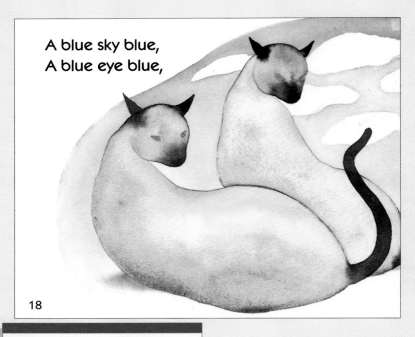

A blue sky blue,
A blue eye blue,

18

QuickREFERENCE

Social Studies Link

Note that the story takes place on a farm. Review the pictures on page 10–11 and pages 16–17. Have children use both spreads to identify things found on the farm. Discuss what they could expect to find in the city, by contrast.

MEETING INDIVIDUAL NEEDS **Challenge**

Have children look at pages 16–17 and name the animals they see in the background. (rabbit, cat, frog, turtle) Ask them how these background details help to make the scene more interesting and realistic.

Now who said blue?
Could it be you?

17

19

Math Link

Ask children to count the cats they
see. How many are there? (three)
How many clouds are in the sky?
(six) You might like to use
manipulatives to demonstrate that
six is equal to two sets of three.

Concepts About Print

Directionality/ Return Sweep

Teach/Model

TESTED SKILL

Reread the question
on page 16, sweeping
your hand under the
words as you read them from left
to right. Then invite several
children to do the same thing as
they and you read again.

Then show children that when you
come to the next line of print, you
must go all the way to the left
again to find the beginning of the
sentence and then read toward
the right. Read the question once
again and then go immediately
into the response, sweeping from
left to right as you read the words.

Follow a similar procedure to
model how to read the two lines
on page 18. Then have volunteers
run their hands under the lines to
show where they would begin to
read, and how they would make
the return sweep.

Practice/Apply

Have children take turns following
your model of the return sweep as
you display pages 6–7 and
10–11 of the story.

SKILL FINDER *Fun with Sentence Strips,*
page T174

Interact *with* **Literature**

20

22

(Math Link)

Ask children to point to something that is both blue and round on page 21. (ball)

Students Acquiring English

MEETING INDIVIDUAL NEEDS

Word Meaning Show children a bow in someone's shoelace. Then have them find all the bows in the picture on page 20. Use lengths of string or yarn to demonstrate how to tie a bow and have children practice.

A bow, a ball, a blue jean blue.

21

Well hello, yellow....
Bright and mellow.

23

Word Meaning Ask children to point out what is blue jean blue on page 21. Help children understand that the boy's overalls are made out of denim, the same material as blue jeans. Ask children who are wearing blue jeans to stand up.

Phonemic Awareness Review

Reread page 23. Ask children to listen for words that rhyme. *(yellow, mellow)* If children ask, tell them that *mellow* means a soft, warm quality and that here it describes the color yellow.

Interact
with
Literature

Reading Strategies

▶ **Think About Words**

Ask children how they could figure out the meaning of *slicker* on page 24 if they didn't know the word.

What makes sense I know that this word names something that is usually yellow.

Picture clues In the picture, I see children wearing yellow hats and coats. One child has an umbrella, and there are puddles on the ground, so it must have just stopped raining. I think a slicker is raincoat.

Slicker yellow,
Sunshine yellow,

24

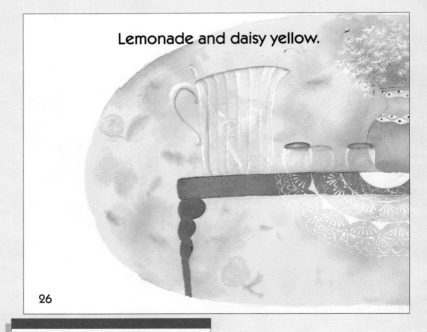

Lemonade and daisy yellow.

26

Quick**REFERENCE**

Visual Literacy

Ask children if they notice anything special about the girl's umbrella. Point out the duck handle and mention that it is just perfect on an umbrella since ducks like water, which rolls right off their feathers.

Extra Support

Word Meaning Many children will need to be told that a slicker is a special kind of raincoat. It is smooth and shiny and the rain just rolls off it.

25

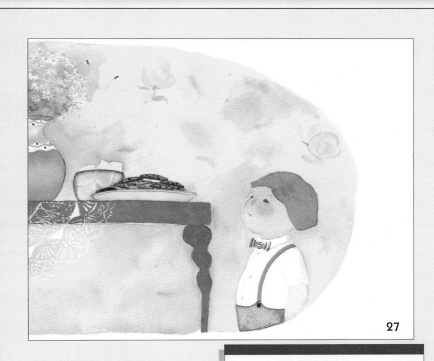

27

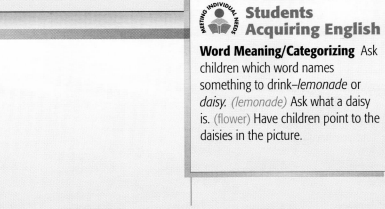

Students Acquiring English

MEETING INDIVIDUAL NEEDS

Word Meaning/Categorizing Ask children which word names something to drink–*lemonade* or *daisy. (lemonade)* Ask what a daisy is. *(flower)* Have children point to the daisies in the picture.

Interact
with
Literature

Reading Strategies

▶ **Evaluate**

Student Application Ask children if they think the color game the girl and boy are playing is a good way to spend a day. Would they like to play the game, too? Encourage children to explain their thinking.

QuickREFERENCE

Visual Literacy

Help children understand that the pictures show the girl and boy moving farther and farther away from the farm each time they talk about another color. Help them compare pages 28–29 and 30–31, noting that on the latter pages the cow is in the background. The girl and boy have moved on to a new place.

Not purple, then,
Or brown or pink...,

29

Tell me, again,
Just what you said.

31

 Multicultural Link

Tell children that people all over the world enjoy flying kites. Some places even have a special kite holiday. In China, it is called Kites Day. In Japan, it is called Children's Day.

Comprehension

 TESTED SKILL

Inferences: Drawing Conclusions

Teach/Model

Remind children that no matter what color the girl talks about, her brother keeps repeating that he "said red." Model thinking about why he is so interested only in red.

Think Aloud

All through the story, the boy thinks only about "red," even though his sister likes to talk about green, blue, and other colors. Finally, the boy finds a red kite. I think he has been looking for it all along. He may have asked his sister to help him find it. While they were looking in many different places, she thought it would be fun to think about all kinds of things that come in all kinds of colors.

Practice/Apply

Have children talk about how the red kite might have gotten into the bush. Offer prompts, as needed:

- Did someone hide it there?
- Did the wind blow it away from the boy?
- Did he leave the kite there the last time he played with it?

Encourage children to tell why they think as they do.

 SKILL FINDER

Drawing Conclusions, page T172

Minilessons: Themes 5, 7, 12

Interact with Literature

Reading Strategies

▶ **Evaluate**

Student Application Encourage children to tell if they think the events in this story could happen in real life. Have them explain their thinking. Then ask how many children would recommend this story to friends. Have those children tell why.

Did you say red?

YES, I SAID RED!

32

Self-Assessment

Ask children how they help themselves while reading. Encourage them to ask themselves:

● Did I understand everything I read in this story? Could I tell a friend what this story was mostly about?

Quick**REFERENCE**

Visual Literacy

Ask children if they think the boy can reach his kite easily. Point out that the artist has drawn him stretching his arms way up to reach and standing on tip toes. Invite children to stand on tip toes and reach way up high overhead.

2

Interact with Literature

Rereading

Literacy Activity Book, p. 23

red	brown
yellow	white
green	black
blue	pink

Who said _____?

_____

I said _____!

Who Said Red? LANGUAGE PATTERNS
Read aloud the color words with children. Then have them write the word that names a color from the story to complete the sentences. Invite them to draw a picture of something that usually that color.

Color is Everywhere

Choices for Rereading

Recognizing Language Patterns

LAB, p. 23

After rereading *Who Said Red?,* reinforce its language pattern. Lead children in the following chant:

> Teacher: Who said red?
>
> Children: I said red.
>
> Teacher: Did *you* say red?
>
> Child 1: Strawberry red.
>
> Child 2: Lollipop red.
>
> Child 3: Fire engine red.

Continue to invite volunteers to name different kinds of red. Repeat the chant for other colors.

Then have children complete the sentences on *Literacy Activity Book,* page 23, with the name of a color they like. They can draw a picture of something that color and then write or dictate something about their picture.

Cooperative Reading

As you reread the story, have children chime in every time the little brother says "I SAID RED!" Clue children by providing the first word (YES or NO) of what the boy says. Then motion for children to join in. Encourage them to try to communicate the boy's feelings as they say the words.

Developing an Ear for Colors

To encourage careful listening, reread the story, occasionally substituting items for those named for a particular color. Tell children to call out "Stop!" each time they hear a "blooper," such as "A strawberry green."

Informal Assessment

Use the Choices for Rereading and Choices for Responding to assess children's general understanding of the story. Also note their ability to recognize that print is read from top to bottom.

Responding

Choices for Responding

Felt Board Retelling

Prepare a felt board color chart for children. Use a black felt background and create columns for each of the different colors. Mark each column with a felt square of red, green, blue, or yellow. Then cut felt shapes for the following:

red	green	blue	yellow
Santa hat	frog	ball	rain slicker
fire engine	tree	blue jeans	sun
cherry	green bean	bow	daisy

Arrange the shapes in piles by color. Then have pairs of children use the shapes to retell the story. For example:

Child 1: Who said red?

Child 2: Did you say red? (picking up cherry) A cherry is red.

Story Talk

Have small groups of children talk together about these questions:

- Why do you think the girl made up the color game to play with her brother while they looked for the kite?

- How do you think the girl feels about her brother? How do you think he feels about playing the color game?

- Would you like to be friends with the children in the story? Why or why not?

Colorful Expressions

Have children each select a color that was featured in the story. Invite children to create drawings of items named in the story for their selected color. Help children label their pictures with the color name.

Suggest that children use their pictures to share the story with their families.

Portfolio Opportunity

Save *Literacy Activity Book,* page 23, as a record of children's ability to work with the language pattern in the story.

3 Instruct *and* Integrate

Comprehension

Literacy Activity Book, p. 24

Practice Activities

Drawing Conclusions

LAB, p. 24

Extra Support Review with children why the boy in the story was so interested in the color red. Ask if they think it's because:

- his hair is red,
- his kite is red,
- red is his favorite color.

Discuss that while any of these *may* be reasons, the most likely one is that he wants his red kite, which is stuck in a bush.

Then talk with children about why the girl in the story kept naming other colors. Was she playing a game with her brother? Was she teasing him, perhaps? Where did she get the idea for each new color she named?

Have children complete *Literacy Activity Book,* page 24.

Concluding Questions

Ask children to listen carefully as you read aloud two statements. Read:

- All fruits have seeds.
- Strawberries are fruits.

Then ask:

- Do strawberries have seeds?

Help children conclude that strawberries must have seeds, since they are fruits.

Repeat with the following statements:

- Some slickers are yellow.
- I have a slicker.
- Is my slicker yellow?

Farm Questions

Display the title page or pages 10–11 of *Who Said Red?* Help children draw conclusions about life on a farm by asking:

- Why are farms usually out in the country rather than in the city? (There's more open land in the country; farm animals like cows need open land for grazing.)

- What do you think the red building— the barn—is for? (Some farm animals are probably kept in the building at night.)

- Why is there a fenced-in area beside the barn on this farm? (to keep animals from wandering off)

Informal Assessment

As children complete the activities, note their ability to draw appropriate conclusions.

Concept Development

Practice Activities

A World of Colors

LAB, p. 25

Extra Support If possible, take children outdoors to do this activity. If that's not practical, they can look out a window.

Remind children that the girl in *Who Said Red?* got her ideas for new colors to name by looking at the world around her. Ask children to look around and to get an idea for a color word from something they see. Ask a volunteer to act as the leader and to name the color of something he or she sees. Other children should hold up crayons of that color and then use them to draw pictures of things they see of that color.

Have children compare their pictures. Ask the leaders which ones show what he or she was thinking of.

Repeat the activity several times, with new leaders and new colors. Then have children complete *Literacy Activity Book,* page 25.

Materials
- box of crayons for each child
- drawing paper

Literacy Activity Book, p. 25

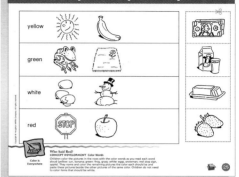

Color Wheels

- Cut out six wedges of colored construction paper: red, blue, yellow, green, orange, and purple.

- Glue the wedges to a large disk of poster board. Label each wedge.

- Have children match the colors of small objects or magazine pictures to each wheel.

Questions and Answers

Listen to the tape "What Is Pink?" to explore the concept of questions and answers. Write the question *What Is Pink?* on the board. Point out the question mark and explain that it signals a question.

Tell children that when we ask a question, we expect an answer. Have children suggest answers to the question. Record their answers on the board.

Reread *Who Said Red?* with children. Tell them to raise their hands each time they hear a question.

Portfolio Opportunity

Save *Literacy Activity Book,* page 25, as a record of children's ability to recognize color words. As children complete the Comprehension activities, write down some observations about each child's ability to draw conclusions. Place the observations in their portfolios.

Instruct *and* Integrate

Concepts About Print

Practice Activities

Fun with Sentence Strips

 Extra Support Make sentence strips for pages 30-31 of *Who Said Red?* Use a different color marker to write each line, in this order: orange, black, blue, purple. (This will help children identify the lines.)

Display pages 30-31, sweeping your hands under the words as you reread the text. Then distribute the sentence strips to four children and have them put them in a pocket chart—in order to make the text on pages 30-31.

Ask a child to come to the pocket chart and show:

- where to begin reading (at the top or with the orange line; on the left)

- how to read this line (from left to right)

- what line to read next (the second line or with the black line)

- *where* to begin reading that line (at the left)

Continue by having other children come to the chart to show how to continue reading. Then invite children to read the lines along with you.

> **Not orange, or black**
>
> **Or white, I think.**
>
> **Tell me, again,**
>
> **Just what you said.**

> We like red and blue and green and pink and purple.

We Know What We Like...

Tape a sheet of white paper to the chalkboard. Hold it vertically so that you will need to make a return sweep while writing a sentence. Print *We like* in fairly large letters at the top. Ask children to take turns naming their favorite colors. As children name the colors, print the color words, joined by *and*.

As you write, point out that we write letters from left to right, and that when we run out of room on a line, we move back to the left side and begin again.

And We Like What We Know!

Display the sentence created in the activity "We Know What We Like." Ask volunteers to come to the board and show how to read this sentence. Encourage children to run their hands under the words as they read them.

Give each child a 3" x 5" index card. Tell them to copy the sentence about colors they like onto their cards. As children are writing, be sure that they move from left to right and make the return sweep when they run out of room on a line.

Informal Assessment

- As children complete the activities on this page, check that they understand how to make the return sweep while reading and writing.

- As children complete the listening activities, note whether they have developed good listening skills.

Listening

Listening Activities

Listen and Read!

 Audio Tape for Color Is Everywhere: *Who Said Red?*

In the Reading/Listening Center, place copies of the Little Big Book together with the Audio Tape for *Who Said Red?* As children listen to the tape, they can run their hands under the lines to show their understanding of left-to-right progression and return sweep.

Roses Are Red

Display the poster for "Roses Are Red." Reread the rhyme with children. Ask children to listen for two words that rhyme. *(blue, you)*

Ask children to listen as you say a few other words. They should raise their hands if a word rhymes with *blue* and *you.* Say: *do, rose, too, new,* and *sad.*

Challenge Children might use one of the rhyming words to dictate a new line for the poem.

Listen to a Story

Share with children a typical pourquoi story about an animal and how it got its color. (Children will later write such stories of their own, so this will serve as a model.) You might choose one or more stories from a book of pourquoi tales.

Children will delight in hearing how the tiger got its stripes or how the peacock got its bright feathers.

Are You Listening?

Recall with children that in *Who Said Red?* the girl doesn't seem to be listening when her brother says "NO, I SAID RED!" Ask children to help you think of some "rules" for good listening.

You may want to remind children that when they cross a street they should do three things: STOP, LOOK, LISTEN. You can use this slogan to help make a "Rules for Listening" chart.

Display the chart in the classroom. Review the rules frequently with children.

RULES FOR LISTENING
STOP what you are doing.
LOOK at who is talking.
LISTEN with both ears!

Instruct *and* Integrate

Independent Reading & Writing

Magic Paint
illustrated by
Robin Spowart

This story provides an independent reading experience with theme content and concepts.

INTERACTIVE LEARNING

Independent Reading
Watch Me Read

Preview and Predict
- Display *Magic Paint.* Point to and read the title.
- Briefly discuss the cover illustration with children. Invite them to predict what this book might be about.
- Tell children that since this book has no words, they will need to look carefully at the pictures to tell the story.

Telling the Story
- The wordless book, *Magic Paint,* will provide children with an independent book experience. Encourage children to tell the story to themselves as they look at each picture to see if their predictions about *Magic Paint* are correct.
- After completing the story, ask:

  Which animal has to jump highest to paint its color?

  Which animal takes the lowest jump to paint its color?

  What do all the animals do at the end of the story?

Choices for Rereading
- **Tell It to a Friend** Suggest that children take turns telling the story to classmates or to adults in the classroom.
- **Concept Review** Have children look at the pictures and name the colors they see. You might want to call out a color name and have children look only for that color. Then repeat with other color names.

Choices for Responding
- **Personal Response** Invite children to tell what they liked best about the book.
- **Act It Out** Invite children to act out different scenes from the story. You might suggest that they use pantomime—a perfect vehicle for a wordless story.

Informal Assessment

- As children tell the *Magic Paint* story, note their use of story-like language and their ability to use pictures to tell a story.
- As children read on their own, assess their ability to turn pages in sequence.
- As children complete the writing activities, assess their ability to generate ideas for writing topics.

Student-Selected Reading

Let's Look at Books

Display the Big Books *Rain* and *Who Said Red?* in the Reading and Listening Center. Encourage children to read these books aloud with partners. Children may also enjoy reading the books independently. Invite them to do so!

Display the Books for the Library Corner suggested in the Bibliography on page T98. Encourage children to explore these books during scheduled reading times as well as during their leisure time.

Sharing and Reflecting

Schedule times when children can share favorite stories. Encourage children to be creative—and to try to use COLOR—as they share their excitement over a book they have heard or read.

- Make stick puppets to show characters.
- Create little "stage sets" to show story settings.

Student-Selected Writing

Sharing Ideas

Children might begin to draw pictures for story ideas in their journals. They can also brainstorm ideas with partners or in small groups. If children still have difficulty generating ideas, suggest that they write new versions of stories they've heard or read.

Story-Idea Walls

Display in the Writing Center any word webs, labeled pictures, or completed class stories. Encourage children to refer to these for help in generating both topic and word ideas.

Books for Independent Reading

Encourage children to choose their own books. They might choose one of the following titles.

Magic Paint
illustrated by Robin Spowart

Rain
by Robert Kalan

Who Said Red?
by Mary Serfozo

Have pairs of students share the reading of these. Some children may be able to read them independently.

See the Bibliography on pages T98–T99 for more theme-related books for independent reading.

Ideas for Independent Writing

Encourage children to write on self-selected topics. For those who need help getting started, suggest one of the following activities:

- an **invitation** to a birthday party
- a weather **chart**
- a color **book**

Portfolio Opportunity

Save examples of stories children have written or dictated. You might make copies of class stories for each child's portfolio. If possible, highlight the child's contribution to the story.

Instruct *and* **Integrate**

Oral Language

Choices for Oral Language

Colors and Feelings

Display several sheets of colored construction paper. Point to a blue sheet, and ask if children have ever heard the expression "I feel blue." Ask what they think this expression means. Elicit that when people say they feel blue, it means they feel sad.

Discuss other feelings associated with the colors on display. Then ask each child to choose a color, draw a picture using only that color, and try to express how that color makes them feel.

Tear-and-Take Story
LAB, pp. 27–28

Have children remove *Literacy Activity Book* pages 27–28, fold it to make a book, and tell the story to you.

Home Connection Encourage children to take the story home to share it with family members.

> Time for Color

A Play About Colors

Invite children to put on a play about colors. Each child should choose a color to "impersonate." Children might dress in the colors they've chosen or make "sandwich boards" for their colors for children to wear.

Allow children to use their own creative imaginations to come up with the content for the play. They might

- Pretend to be fruits or vegetables or other foods of various colors.

- Think about the feelings colors evoke, and move creatively as appropriate music is played to show those feelings.

Picture This!

Suggest that children choose a favorite scene from *Who Said Red?* and use that scene to prompt a new story. Children can work in small groups to brainstorm story ideas. They can then tell their story to classmates. To get children started, you might display the pictures on the following pages and ask:

- Pages 6-7: Where do you think the fire engine is going? Why is Santa "hitching" a ride on the back?

- Pages 24-25: Who are these children? Where are they going? What are they doing to have fun?

Informal Assessment

- Note children's contributions to the oral language activities.
- As children work on their writing assignments, note their ability to recognize colors and objects associated with that color.

Writing

Choices for Writing

Making a Big Book

MEETING INDIVIDUAL NEEDS

Extra Support Invite children to create a class *Big Book of Color.*

- Choose a color from the poem "What Is Pink?" Brainstorm with children a list of objects associated with that color.

- Have children choose something from the list to draw. Ask them to write or dictate labels for their drawings.

- Staple all drawings for a particular color together to form a booklet. Then staple each booklet to a large sheet of appropriately colored construction paper. At the top, print the question: What is (color name)?

- Combine all color sections to make a Big Book. Add a white construction paper cover. Punch holes at the top and bind with metal rings.

- Print the title on the cover. Then invite children to use different colored crayons to print their names as authors. Add the book to the classroom library.

Self-Portraits

Supply each child with a wide variety of colors (crayons or markers). Have children draw pictures of themselves.

As children are drawing, circulate and ask each child to dictate a few sentences about himself or herself. Children might tell about favorite colors or about things they like to do. Print each child's responses on a large index card and attach it to the drawing the child has made.

Display children's portraits in the Art Gallery.

A Present of Roses

Display the poster for "Roses Are Red." Point out that roses can be pink, yellow, orange, and white—as well as red. Then invite children to draw pictures of their favorite color of roses. They can then write, or dictate, a few words below their pictures.

Remind children that in the first story in this theme—*Mr. Rabbit and the Lovely Present*—the little girl needed a present for her mother. Encourage children to give their pictures away as presents.

**Instruct
and
Integrate**

Cross-Curricular Activities

Music

Mary Wore Her Red Dress

Children may enjoy learning this traditional song/chant. Teach children the following lyrics:

> Mary wore her red dress,
> red dress, red dress,
> Mary wore her red dress
> all day long.

Then, invite children to create new verses for the song by replacing the child's name and the color and type of clothing, for example:

> Ricky wore his green cap,
> green cap, green cap,
> Ricky wore his green cap
> all day long.

Choices for Art

Drips and Dribbles

Children may enjoy experimenting with a variety of painting techniques, such as painting with string, using a paintbrush to dribble and splash, and using a toothbrush to spatter paint onto paper.

Paper Kites

Challenge Ask children to point out the kite on the cover of *Who Said Red?* Then invite them to design their own kites, using brightly colored construction paper to make the body and the tail. Encourage children to decorate their kites with markers or crayons. Display children's kites in the Art Gallery.

Math

Making a Color Graph

Using chart paper and colored stickers, invite children to help you make a graph of the class's favorite colors.

- Ask children to name their favorite colors.

- For each response, mark the graph with a colored sticker or circle.

- Have children visually estimate which color has been chosen most often. Help children count to confirm their estimate.

Discuss how making charts can help us keep track of information.

red	●	●	○	○	○	○	○	○
orange	●	○	○	○	○	○	○	○
yellow	○	○	○	○	○	○	○	○
green	●	●	●	●	○	○	○	○
blue	●	●	●	○	○	○	○	○
purple	●	●	○	○	○	○	○	○
pink	●	○	○	○	○	○	○	○
brown	○	○	○	○	○	○	○	○

Social Studies

Seeing Red

Discuss with children that stop signs and stop lights are always red. Point out that the color red on something is often a signal to pay special attention. Display the Signs of Color poster and invite children to identify the objects and their colors, encouraging them to talk about why they think the objects are those colors. Have children name other places where red is used as a way to get attention. Children may suggest such things as flashing lights on police patrol cars and red fire extinguishers.

Poster

Signs of Color

Poster: Color Is Everywhere

Theme Assessment Wrap-Up

ASSESSMENT

Reflecting/Self-Assessment

Copy the chart below to distribute to children. Ask them which stories in the theme they liked best. Then discuss what was easy for them and what was more difficult as they read the selections and completed the activities. Have children put a check mark under either *Easy* or *Hard.*

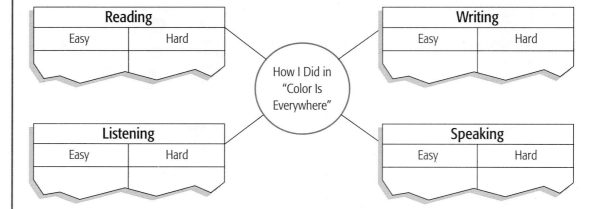

Reading	
Easy	Hard

Writing	
Easy	Hard

How I Did in "Color Is Everywhere"

Listening	
Easy	Hard

Speaking	
Easy	Hard

Monitoring Literacy Development

There will be many opportunities to observe and evaluate children's literacy development. As children participate in literacy activities, note whether each child has a beginning, a developing, or a proficient understanding of reading, writing, and language concepts. The Observation Checklists, which can be used for recording and evaluating this information, appear in the *Teacher's Assessment Handbook.* They are comprised of the following:

Concepts About Print and Book Handling Behaviors

- Concepts about print
- Book handling

Emergent Reading Behaviors

- Responding to literature
- Storybook rereading
- Decoding strategies

Emergent Writing Behaviors

- Writing
- Stages of temporary spelling

Oral Language Behaviors

- Listening attentively
- Listening for information
- Listening to directions
- Listening to books
- Speaking/language development
- Participating in conversations and discussions

Retelling Behaviors

- Retelling a story
- Retelling informational text

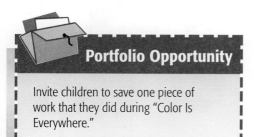

Portfolio Opportunity

Invite children to save one piece of work that they did during "Color Is Everywhere."

Choices for Assessment

Informal Assessment

Review the Observation Checklists and observation notes to determine:

- Did children's responses during and after reading indicate comprehension of the selections?

- How well did children understand the skills presented in this theme? Which skills should be reviewed and practiced in the next theme?

- Did children enjoy the cooperative activities related to the major theme concept?

Formal Assessment

Select formal tests that meet your class-room needs:

- *Kindergarten Literacy Survey*
- Theme Skills Test for "Color Is Everywhere"

See the *Teacher's Assessment Handbook* for guidelines for administering tests and using answer keys and children's sample papers.

Portfolio Assessment

Selecting Materials for the Portfolio

Tell the children that you will sometimes have them put special work in the portfolio. Explain to them that together you will be able to look at the work and watch as they change as learners. Tell them that they may also put special pieces in the portfolio. If they have something special to put in, they should let you know.

Be sure to make a couple of portfolio selections from each theme. Try to vary what you choose. Use the Portfolio icons in the lower left corner of the *Teacher's Book* to help you know which *Literacy Activity Book* pages and activities might be good portfolio entries. Do not use all the suggestions; select a few.

Managing Assessment
Communicating with Parents

Question: How can I communicate with parents?

Answer: Try these suggestions:

- Use the parent newsletters that accompany each theme to help parents know what children will be reading and learning.

- Even though you will be keeping a portfolio, try to send some work home at least once a week. The Tear-and-Take and Watch Me Read books and many of the *Literacy Activity Book* pages will help parents understand what their children are learning.

- Discuss, model, and practice with children how to tell their parents what they are learning in school. Have them role-play. Make this a regular part of each theme.

For more information on this and other topics, see the *Teacher's Assessment Handbook*.

Celebrating the Theme

Choices for Celebrating

Materials

- **Read Aloud Book:** *Mr. Rabbit and the Lovely Present*
- **Big Books:** *Rain* and *Who Said Red?*
- **Watch Me Read:** *Magic Paint*

See the **Houghton Mifflin Internet** resources for additional theme-related activities.

Self-Assessment

Have children meet in small groups to discuss what they learned in the theme. Use the following prompts to foster their discussion:

- Which selection in the theme did you like best? Why?
- Name some of your favorite colors and some things that are those colors.

Book Talk

Display the theme books, and ask children to talk about which one they liked best and why. Then, group children according to their favorite story. Give the appropriate book to each group. Invite children to take turns retelling the story.

Theme Talk

Ask children to talk about what they learned during this theme. Encourage them to share their feelings about the poems you have read together and any songs they may have sung. Discuss what children have learned about colors, including color names, things that are each color, and what happens when colors are mixed together.

Come to the Art Gallery!

Help children plan for the official "opening" of their Art Gallery. Children can make announcements of the opening to be sent home to parents and/or to other classes. Ask children to check to be sure that their names are on all the pieces of art that they have contributed. As visitors tour the gallery, children can tell about the things they've made—and learned—during the *Color Is Everywhere* theme.

Teacher's Handbook

TABLE OF CONTENTS

Story Retelling Props

Materials
- oaktag
- crayons or markers
- scissors

On Monday When It Rained

Children can use a cardboard frame to help them show the feelings of the boy in *On Monday When It Rained.* To make the frame, cut a 16" square from heavy cardboard or oaktag. Then cut out the center of the square leaving a 2" border that could be decorated. Have children hold up the frame and make faces to show the boy's different feelings. Invite other children in the group to guess what feelings are being expressed.

Resources
- 26 stick-on letters
- prop board

ABC and You

To retell *ABC and You,* lay out the stick-on letters and lean the prop board against the chalkboard or an easel. Then invite a child to pick out a stick-on letter and put it in its outlined place on the prop board. The child should say the letter, and then say a describing word and a name: "G — Graceful Georgiana," for example. Children take turns, using the names from the story, their own names, or other names. When all the letters are on the prop board, the class can say the whole alphabet in order together.

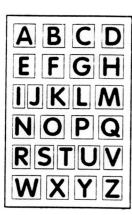

INTERACTIVE LEARNING *(continued)*

ABC and You

Children will enjoy using a set of alphabet cards to retell *ABC and You.* Make them by writing one capital letter on each of twenty-six 3″ x 5″ index cards or oaktag rectangles. To help children with letter orientation, draw a line beneath each letter. Put the cards in alphabetical order in a basket or small box. Invite children to pick one card, say the letter, and then say a describing word and a name.

Materials
- 26 3″ x 5″ cards
- marker or crayon

Faces

This prop can help children recall the language patterns used in the book *Faces.* Draw five oval shapes about the size of a child's face onto two 11″ x 17″ pieces of oaktag taped end to end. In the oval on the left, cut a hole for a mouth; on the next oval cut a hole for a nose, then two eye holes, two ear holes, and then cut out the fifth oval completely. Children can hold up the ovals, showing the appropriate parts of their faces. Help them recall some of the phrases about parts of faces that were featured in the book.

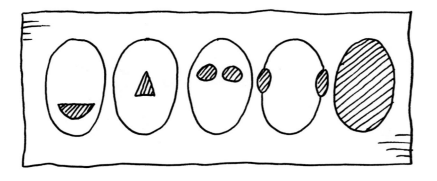

Materials
- 11″ x 17″ oaktag sheets
- pencil or pen
- scissors

Story Retelling Props

Resources
- puppets
- stick-on retelling pieces
- prop board

Mr. Rabbit and the Lovely Present

Children will enjoy manipulating the puppets and the stick-on retelling pieces to act out this story. Lean the prop board against an easel or chalkboard. Demonstrate how to work the puppets by slipping your thumb and forefinger through the slots in one of them. Then guide pairs of children as they role-play the scenes from the story and place the stick-on pieces where they belong on the prop board. Encourage the children to model their dialogue on the patterns from the book.

Materials
- old socks
- yarn
- buttons
- construction paper
- glue

Mr. Rabbit and the Lovely Present

Make puppets from old socks to retell *Mr. Rabbit and the Lovely Present.* Use glue to attach construction paper, yarn, and buttons for the faces. Children can use the finished hand puppets as they re-create the story dialogue. Help children to make fruit props to enhance the retelling. Draw or cut out pictures of red apples, yellow bananas, green pears, and blue grapes. Glue the fruit pictures to construction paper. You may also want to create props for each of the rejected objects. Encourage children to retell the story by picking up the appropriate pictures and placing them in a basket.

Rain

To help the children retell *Rain,* make a mural with about 6 feet of white craft paper. Divide the paper into three sections from end to end. Have the children help draw or cut and paste clouds in the first section, rain in the second section, and a rainbow in the third section. Hang the mural so the bottom edge is along the floor. Then tape sheets of black construction paper together to make a road that runs from one end of the mural to the other. Children can use a toy car brought from home to roll along the road and recreate the sequence of events in the story.

Materials
● toy car
● roll of craft paper
● construction paper
● crayons or markers
● scissors
● glue

Who Said Red?

For *Who Said Red?* prepare a felt board color chart. Use a black felt background, and create columns marked with a felt square of red, green, blue, and yellow. Then cut felt shapes for the following: red—Santa hat, fire engine, cherry; green—frog, tree, green bean; blue—cloud, bow, blue jeans; yellow—rain slicker, sun, daisy. Arrange the shapes into piles according to their colors. Then guide pairs of children to retell the story. Encourage the children to pattern their dialogue on the wording in the book.

Materials
● felt pieces
● felt board
● scissors

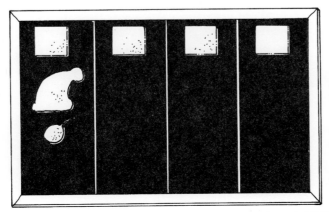

Games

Alphabet Adventure

Players: Two–Four

Resources
- Alphabet Adventure game board
- Tokens

Preparation Have each player choose one different-colored token and place it on the space labeled START.

Directions In turn, each player:

1. Spins the spinner and, when it stops on a color, moves his or her token forward to the first space of that color.

2. Names the letter on that space.

3. Continues playing until one player reaches FINISH. If a player spins to a color that is not ahead of his or her token, the player moves directly to FINISH and wins.

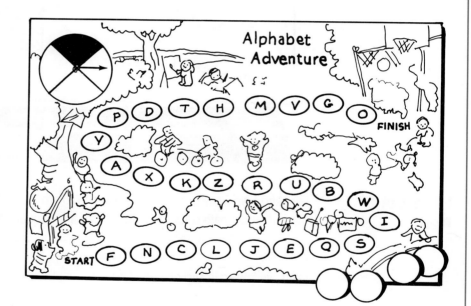

INTERACTIVE LEARNING (continued)

Additional Game Idea: Alphabet Bingo

Players: Two–Four

Here is an additional game idea to reinforce identification of capital letters.

Preparation Make four 6-inch square bingo cards out of tagboard. Divide each card into nine spaces. Print capital letters in random order on each of the four bingo cards, varying the letters on each card. Place the Letter Cards in a pile. Provide children with one-inch paper squares to use as markers.

Directions In turn, each player:

1. Chooses a letter card from the pile.

2. Names the letter and looks on his or her bingo card for a letter that matches the one selected.

3. Places a marker over the square on the bingo card if a match is found.

4. Continues playing until one player covers all letters on his or her bingo card with markers.

Variation Use lowercase Letter Cards *a–z* to provide practice with lowercase letter identification.

Materials
• Letter Cards: *A-Z*
• Tagboard
• Paper squares for markers

Games

Resources
- Color Round the Rhyme game board
- Tokens

Color Round the Rhyme

Players: Two–Four

Preparation Name each picture on the game board with children: *knee, man, cat, hole, tree, van, bat, roll, pea, can, rat, mole, key, pan, mat, pole.* Name each picture on the spinner with children: *bee, hat, fan, bowl.* Have each child choose a group of tokens of one color. The child's token color will also be his or her color section on the game board.

Directions In turn, each player:

1. Spins the spinner.

2. Names the picture shown on the spinner.

3. Looks in his or her color section for a picture with a name that rhymes with the picture on the spinner.

4. Places a token on the picture with a name that rhymes. If a picture has been covered, the player does not put down a token.

5. Continues playing until one player covers all four objects in his or her color section.

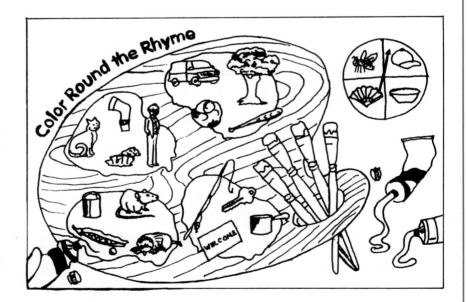

INTERACTIVE LEARNING *(continued)*

Additional Game Idea: Rhyming Puzzles

Players: One or More

Here is an additional game idea to reinforce recognition of rhymes.

Preparation Draw and cut five circles of construction paper in different colors. Cut each circle into two pieces to create a puzzle. On one puzzle piece, draw a picture of a sock. On the other piece, draw a picture of a lock. Create additional puzzles using the following words: *whale/nail, car/star, cat/hat, goat/boat, dish/fish.* Cut the puzzles in a variety of shapes. Name the pictures with children.

Directions Players work individually or in pairs to complete the puzzles by matching the pieces that have rhyming pictures.

Materials
- Five colors of construction paper

If You're Happy and You Know It

If you're hap- py and you know it, clap your hands.

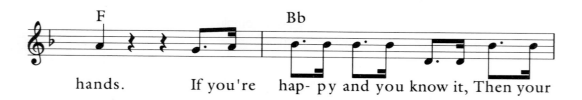

If you're hap- py and you know it, clap your hands.

If you're hap- py and you know it, Then your

face will sure- ly show it, If you're

hap- py and you know it, clap your hands.

ABC Song

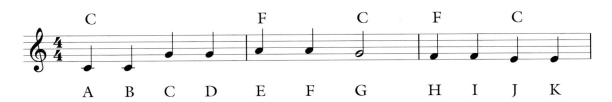

A   B   C   D   E   F   G   H   I   J   K

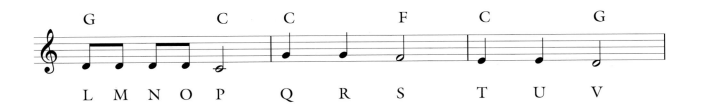

L   M   N   O   P   Q   R   S   T   U   V

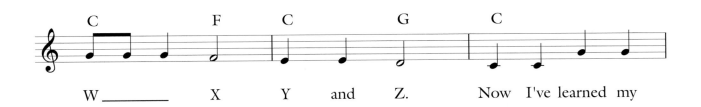

W _____   X   Y   and   Z.   Now I've learned my

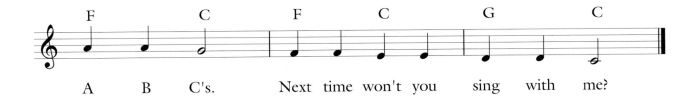

A   B   C's.   Next time won't you sing with me?

I Am Special, I Am Me

DEBORAH K. COYLE

I am spe-cial, I am me, __ I have two hands, two

eyes to see, __ A nose to smell, my ears hear well, __ A

mouth to talk and two legs to walk. But that's not all be-

cause you see, I am spe-cial, I __ am me!

Sing A Rainbow

ARTHUR HAMILTON

Sing a Rainbow (continued)

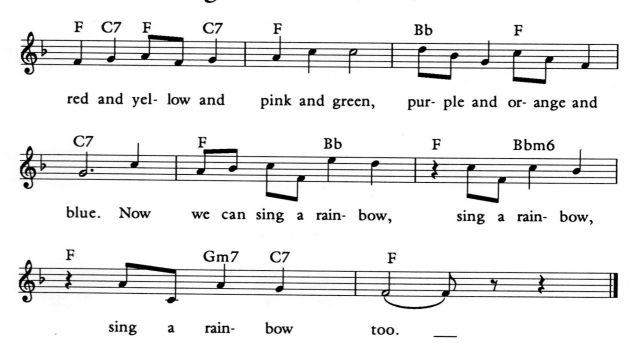

red and yel- low and   pink and green,   pur- ple and or- ange and

blue. Now   we can sing a rain- bow,   sing a rain- bow,

sing   a   rain- bow   too. __

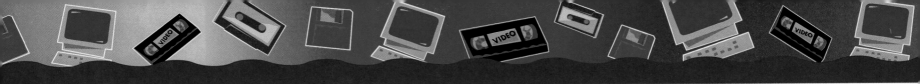

Audio-Visual Resources

Adventure Productions
3404 Terry Lake Road
Ft. Collins, CO 80524

AIMS Media
9710 DeSoto Avenue
Chatsworth, CA
91311-4409
800-367-2467

Alfred Higgins Productions
6350 Laurel Canyon
Blvd.
N. Hollywood, CA
91606
800-766-5353

**American School
Publishers/SRA**
P.O. Box 543
Blacklick, OH
43004-0543
800-843-8855

Audio Bookshelf
R.R. #1, Box 706
Belfast, ME 04915
800-234-1713

Audio Editions
Box 6930
Auburn, CA 95604-6930
800-231-4261

Audio Partners, Inc.
Box 6930
Auburn, CA 95604-6930
800-231-4261

Bantam Doubleday Dell
1540 Broadway
New York, NY 10036
212-782-9652

Barr Films
12801 Schabarum Ave.
Irwindale, CA 97106
800-234-7878

Bullfrog Films
Box 149
Oley, PA 19547
800-543-3764

Churchill Films
12210 Nebraska Ave.
Los Angeles, CA 90025
800-334-7830

Clearvue/EAV
6465 Avondale Ave.
Chicago, IL 60631
800-253-2788

Coronet/MTI
108 Wilmot Road
Deerfield, IL 60015
800-777-8100

Creative Video Concepts
5758 SW Calusa Loop
Tualatin, OR 97062

**Dial Books for Young
Readers**
375 Hudson St.
New York, NY 10014
800-526-0275

Direct Cinema Ltd.
P.O. Box 10003
Santa Monica, CA 90410
800-525-0000

**Disney Educational
Production**
105 Terry Drive,
Suite 120
Newtown, PA 18940
800-295-5010

Encounter Video
2550 NW Usshur
Portland, OR 97210
800-677-7607

Filmic Archives
The Cinema Center
Botsford, CT 06404
800-366-1920

**Films for Humanities and
Science**
P.O. Box 2053
Princeton, NJ 08543
609-275-1400

Finley-Holiday
12607 E. Philadelphia St.
Whittier, CA 90601

Fulcrum Publishing
350 Indiana St.
Golden, CO 80401

G.K. Hall
Box 500, 100 Front St.
Riverside, NJ 08057

HarperAudio
10 East 53rd Street
New York, NY 10022
212-207-6901

Hi-Tops Video
2730 Wiltshire Blvd.
Suite 500
Santa Monica, CA 90403
213-216-7900

Houghton Mifflin/Clarion
Wayside Road
Burlington, MA 01803
800-225-3362

Idaho Public TV/Echo Films
1455 North Orchard
Boise, ID 83706
800-424-7963

Kidvidz
618 Centre St.
Newton, MA 02158
617-965-3345

L.D.M.I.
P.O. Box 1445,
St. Laurent
Quebec, Canada H4L
4Z1

Let's Create
50 Cherry Hill Rd.
Parsippany, NJ 07054

Listening Library
One Park Avenue
Old Greenwich, CT
06870
800-243-4504

Live Oak Media
P.O. Box 652
Pine Plains, NY 12567
518-398-1010

Mazon Productions
3821 Medford Circle
Northbrook, IL 60062
708-272-2824

Media Basics
Lighthouse Square
705 Boston Post Road
Guildford, CT 06437
800-542-2505

MGM/UA Home Video
1000 W. Washington
Blvd.
Culver City, CA 90232
310-280-6000

Milestone Film and Video
275 W. 96th St.,
Suite 28C
New York, NY 10025

Miramar
200 Second Ave.
Seattle, WA 98119
800-245-6472

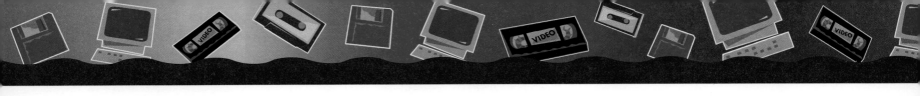

Audio-Visual Resources *(continued)*

National Geographic
Educational Services
Washington, DC 20036
800-548-9797

The Nature Company
P.O. Box 188
Florence, KY 41022
800-227-1114

Philomel
1 Grosset Drive
Kirkwood, NY 13795
800-847-5575

Premiere Home Video
755 N. Highland
Hollywood, CA 90038
213-934-8903

Puffin Books
375 Hudson St.
New York, NY 10014

Rabbit Ears
131 Rowayton Avenue
Rowayton, CT 06853
800-800-3277

Rainbow Educational Media
170 Keyland Court
Bohemia, NY 11716
800-331-4047

Random House Media
400 Hahn Road
Westminster, MD 21157
800-733-3000

Reading Adventure
7030 Huntley Road,
Unit B
Columbus, OH 43229

Recorded Books
270 Skipjack Road
Prince Frederick,
MD 20678
800-638-1304

SelectVideo
7200 E. Dry Creek Rd.
Englewood, CO 80112
800-742-1455

Silo/Alcazar
Box 429, Dept. 318
Waterbury, VT 05676

Spoken Arts
10100 SBF Drive
Pinellas Park, FL 34666
800-126-8090

SRA
P.O. Box 543
Blacklick, OH
43004-0543
800-843-8855

Strand/VCI
3350 Ocean Park Blvd.
Santa Monica, CA 90405
800-922-3827

Taliesin Productions
558 Grove St.
Newton, MA 02162
617-332-7397

Time-Life Education
P.O. Box 85026
Richmond, VA
23285-5026
800-449-2010

Video Project
5332 College Ave.
Oakland, CA 94618
800-475-2638

Warner Home Video
4000 Warner Blvd.
Burbank, CA 91522
818-243-5020

Weston Woods
Weston, CT 06883
800-243-5020

Wilderness Video
P.O. Box 2175
Redondo Beach, CA
90278
310-539-8573

BOOKS AVAILABLE IN SPANISH
Spanish editions of English titles referred to in the Bibliography are available from the following publishers or distributors.

Bilingual Educational Services, Inc.
2514 South Grand Ave.
Los Angeles, CA
90007-9979
800-448-6032

Charlesbridge
85 Main Street
Watertown, MA 02172
617-926-5720

Children's Book Press
6400 Hollis St., Suite 4
Emeryville, CA 94608
510-655-3395

Childrens Press
5440 N. Cumberland
Ave.
Chicago, IL 60656-1469
800-621-1115

Econo-Clad Books
P.O. Box 1777
Topeka, KS 66601
800-628-2410

Farrar, Straus, & Giroux
9 Union Square
New York, NY 10003
212-741-6973

Harcourt Brace
6277 Sea Harbor Drive
Orlando, FL 32887
800-225-5425

HarperCollins
10 E. 53rd Street
New York, NY 10022
717-941-1500

Holiday House
425 Madison Ave.
New York, NY 10017
212-688-0085

Kane/Miller
Box 310529
Brooklyn, NY
11231-0529
718-624-5120

Alfred A. Knopf
201 E. 50th St.
New York, NY 10022
800-638-6460

Lectorum
111 Eighth Ave.
New York, NY 10011
800-345-5946

Santillana
901 W. Walnut St.
Compton, CA 90220
800-245-8584

Simon and Schuster
866 Third Avenue
New York, NY 10022
800-223-2336

Viking
357 Hudson Street
New York, NY 10014
212-366-2000

Index

Boldface page references indicate formal strategy and skill instruction.

T174, T175; *TG4:* **T41, T59**
letter as letter, *TG1:* T39, T54
matches spoken words to print,
TG2: **T133, T147, T167**
middle of sentence, *TG6:* **T73,** T87
recognizing words that are alike,
TG3: **T173, T183;** *TG5:* **T169**
return sweep, *TG1:* **T161,** T174,
T175; *TG2:* **T51**
spoken word as word, *TG2:* **T45**
sentence boundaries, *TG1:* T69,
T76
word boundaries, *TG3:* **T155, T183**
words made of letters, *TG1:* **T39**
words with familiar beginning
sounds, *TG5:* T77, T85, T131,
T133, **T134, T149**
words with familiar ending sounds,
TG5: **T141, T148, T149, T167,
T176**
written word as word, *TG2:* **T75,
T84**

Conclusions, drawing, *TG1:* T46,
T49, **T167, T172;** *TG3:* **T25,** T28;
TG4: **T21, T36,** T40, T44, T52,
T65, T72, T75, T115, T125, T136,
T148, T179; *TG6:* **T121,** T124,
T126. *See also* Inferences, making.

Constructing meaning from text. *See*
Interactive Learning.

Context
clues, *TG1:* T40, T56, T63, T80,
T140; *TG2:* T40, T76, T138,
T160, T166; *TG3:* T22, T44,
T70, T116, T140, T144, T170,
T172; *TG4:* T20, T46, T57, T78,
T138, T172; *TG5:* T22, T38,
T40, T42, T43, T48, T114, T120,
T153; *TG6:* T69, T108
picture clues, *TG1:* T40, T56, T63,
T80, T140; *TG2:* T40, T49, T76,
T138, T160, T166; *TG3:* T18,
T22, T66, T70, T78, T116,
T121, T140, T141, T142, T143,
T144, T170, T171, T172, T180;
TG4: T20, T46, T70, T76, T78,
T138, T172; *TG5:* T22, T38,
T40, T42, T43, T48, T68, T80,
T114, T116, T120, T132, T138,
T153, T164, T181; *TG6:* T22,
T42, T46, T70, T78, T138, T170
using, *TG1:* T30, T56, T63, T80,

T140, T145, T147; *TG2:* T40,
T76, T138, T160, T166; *TG3:*
T22, T44, T70, T116, T140,
T144, T170, T172; *TG4:* T46,
T57, T78, T138, T172; *TG5:* T22,
T38, T40, T42, T43, T48, T68,
T114; *TG6:* T22, T42, T46, T70,
T78, T138, T170
See also Vocabulary, selection.

Cooperative learning activities, *TG1:*
T27, T51, T55, T68, T76, T120,
T141, T171, T177, T178, T184; *TG2:*
T17, T26, T27, T28, T33, T36, T51,
T53, T55, T56, T57, T62, T63, T67,
T77, T84, T85, T89, T91, T94,
T104, T110, T119, T122, T125,
T143, T144, T145, T147, T148, T171,
T172, T178; *TG3:* T27, T36, T37,
T52, T56, T80, T81, T82, T86, T93,
T125, T127, T130, T151, T152,
T156, T178, T179, T181, T182,
T188; *TG4:* T12, T26, T27, T36,
T55, T59, T61, T65, T85, T90, T95,
T96, T97, T121, T125, T139, T153,
T156, T157, T160, T161, T162,
T177, T185, T192, T196, T200;
TG5: T32, T49, T50, T57, T58, T59,
T80, T81, T88, T92, T118, T119,
T120, T122, T145, T146, T150,
T173, T175, T176, T181, T182,
T184; *TG6:* T24, T27, T53, T83,
T87, T125, T126, T160, T195, T196

Cooperative reading. *See* Reading
modes.

Counting, *TG2:* T37, T45, T48, T53,
T54, T55, T57, T58, T66, T75,
T110, T130, T133; *TG4:* T41, T43,
T51, T81, T89, T141, T170, T175.
See also Numbers.

Creative dramatics
acting out scenes, stories, and
words, *TG1:* T17, T22, T26, T86,
T154, T168, T176; *TG2:* T16,
T30, T81, T82, T91; *TG3:* T17,
T27, T80, T124, T150; *TG4:*
T27, T33, T119, T125; *TG5:*
T27; *TG6:* T17, T26, T43, T125,
T153, T200
demonstrating, *TG2:* T19, T22,
T30, T48, T49, T82, T132,
T150; *TG3:* T20, T25, T72, T76,

T78, T90; *TG4:* T18, T42, T71,
T147, T160, T178; *TG5:* T16,
T18, T29, T62, T67, T74, T130,
T152; *TG6:* T24, T41, T45, T46,
T47, T58, T59, T62, T76, T119
dramatizing, *TG1:* T87, T141, T146,
T148, T157; *TG2:* T91; *TG3:*
T124, T150; *TG4:* T26, T27,
T33, T125, T153, T192; *TG5:*
T119, T145, T173
hand/body motions, *TG3:* T90;
TG5: T155; *TG6:* T17, T26,
T185, T195
pantomime, *TG1:* T176; *TG2:* T16,
T23, T119, T142, T153, T183;
TG3: T17, T55, T122, T128,
T150, T188; *TG4:* T26, T54,
T55, T73, T115, T159; *TG5:*
T20, T48, T106, T111; *TG6:*
T53, T112, T125, T138, T191
puppetry, *TG1:* T119, T177; *TG2:*
T77, T81; *TG3:* T80; *TG4:* T58;
TG5: T27
role-playing, *TG1:* T32, T88, T119;
TG2: T19, T26, T33, T119,
T171, T177; *TG3:* T21, T27, T28,
T33, T57, T88, T124, T125,
T148, T157, T185; *TG4:* T30,
T55, T62, T94, T121, T131,
T155, T160; *TG5:* T21, T30,
T47, T49, T87, T122, T145, T173,
T179, T184; *TG6:* T27, T28,
T32, T56, T60, T90, T113, T126
sound effects, *TG3:* T27, T42, T52,
T88; *TG6:* T16, T30, T185

Creative response. *See* Responding to
literature.

Creative thinking, *TG1:* T10, T27,
T51, T81, T89, T90, T102, T119,
T122, T146, T147, T177; *TG2:* T12,
T26, T28, T31, T32, T50, T61, T80,
T82, T131, T142, T180; *TG3:* T25,
T28, T30, T52, T62, T74, T125,
T128, T130, T134, T185, T188,
T189; *TG4:* T27, T30, T31, T32,
T33, T94, T96, T97, T161, T185;
TG5: T17, T27, T37, T54, T59, T82,
T87, T90, T119, T122, T146, T159,
T173, T179, T182; *TG6:* T12, T30,
T31, T32, T37, T52, T53, T54, T63,
T67, T89, T106, T125, T126, T128,
T129, T135, T154, T160, T162,

T166, T167, T192, T194, T195,
T197, T200

Creative writing. *See* Writing,
creative.

Critical thinking, *TG1:* T10, T19, T28,
T43, T45, T52, T69, T82, T102,
T167, T172; *TG2:* T56, T162, T163;
TG3: T12, T17, T18, T20, T24, T27,
T28, T33, T36, T37, T38, T46, T50,
T53, T54, T59, T61, T62, T63, T74,
T75, T78, T81, T82, T87, T88, T111,
T113, T118, T119, T151, T164,
T171, T173, T179; *TG4:* T21, T36,
T40, T44, T52, T65, T81, T97, T114,
T115, T154; *TG5:* T18, T19, T20,
T23, T27, T42, T46, T49, T64, T66,
T70, T72, T137, T143, T145, T154,
T161; *TG6:* T16, T31, T32, T43,
T54, T62, T66, T80, T84, T92,
T106, T125, T131, T153, T156,
T157, T158, T159, T174, T186

Cross-cultural connections. *See*
Multicultural activities.

Cross-curricular activities
art, *TG1:* T28, T33, T51, T59, T69,
T70, T81, T89, T90, T98, T104,
T109, T113, T117, T120, T122,
T123, T125, T142, T143, T144,
T146, T148, T149, T173, T179,
T180, T184; *TG2:* T12, T21,
T25, T28, T29, T31, T32, T37,
T55, T57, T61, T63, T67, T91,
T94, T113, T120, T123, T125,
T132, T143, T148, T151, T171,
T172, T174, T176, T178, T180,
T181, T182, T183; *TG3:* T16,
T57, T62, T131, T160, T161,
T191; *TG4:* T7, T31, T55, T64,
T68, T85, T92, T94, T97, T100,
T125, T129, T131, T135, T153,
T161, T163, T167, T197; *TG5:*
T6, T33, T91, T92, T122, T125,
T154, T184; *TG6:* T24, T62,
T108, T162, T197
health, *TG2:* T6, T90, T98, T113;
TG3: T77, T146, T191; *TG4:* T7,
T44; *TG5:* T18, T44, T59, T132;
TG6 T32, T59:
math, *TG1:* T7, T19, T32, T39, T42,
T44, T59, T68, T73, T74, T90,
T98, T124, T144, T161, T162,

T181; *TG2:* T6, T17, T23, T33,
T37, T39, T44, T45, T46, T50,
T52, T53, T55, T62, T79, T83,
T90, T98, T99, T110, T130,
T153, T165, T166; *TG3:* T32,
T41, T43, T62, T92, T130, T141,
T174; *TG4:* T7, T32, T41, T43,
T96, T104, T130, T162, T170,
T175, T196; *TG5:* T7, T39, T59,
T71, T93, T112, T124, T131,
T142, T155, T184; *TG6:* T33,
T38, T95, T130, T136, T163,
T179, T196
media literacy, *TG1:* T132; *TG2:*
T43, T131; *TG6:* T148
movement, *TG1:* T47, T58; *TG2:*
T26, T124, T153, T183; *TG3:*
T33, T63; *TG4:* T33, T42, T64;
TG5: T58, T155; *TG6:* T17, T26,
T53, T58, T119, T125, T185,
T200
multicultural, *TG1:* T6, T7, T70,
T98, T99, T110, T116, T138,
T145, T167; *TG2:* T24, T75,
T98, T99, T110, T112, T113,
T114, T124, T152; *TG3:* T18,
T39, T49, T119, T147, T190;
TG4: T6, T7, T19, T49, T76,
T104, T105, T117, T130, T169,
T180; *TG5:* T6, T7, T45, T65,
T68, T125, T141, T142; *TG6:*
T66, T68, T70, T72, T74, T76,
T131, T170
music, *TG1:* T12, T16, T29, T33,
T36, T99, T108, T180; *TG2:* T7,
T32, T50, T62, T124; *TG3:* T63,
T93, T114, T139, T161; *TG4:*
T7, T33, T64, T96, T197; *TG5:*
T6, T7, T45, T65, T68, T141,
T142; *TG6:* T17, T26, T63, T196
science, *TG1:* T6, T18, T39, T45,
T46, T64, T65, T66, T75, T91,
T98, T111, T112, T113, T124,
T125, T130, T134, T139, T148,
T155, T156, T159; *TG2:* T6, T7,
T42, T45, T46, T63, T98, T99,
T125, T131, T133, T134, T135,
T136, T138, T139, T141, T149,
T152, T162, T164, T182; *TG3:*
T19, T23, T25, T32, T41, T43,
T47, T62, T63, T77, T93, T115,
T130, T140, T141, T143, T144,
T160, T169, T173, T190; *TG4:*

T7, T23, T46, T65, T72, T75,
T78, T97, T105, T116, T131,
T145, T163, T171, T173, T179;
TG5: T21, T22, T32, T41, T43,
T64, T66, T69, T74, T76, T92,
T113, T115, T116, T124, T136,
T138, T139, T140, T142, T154;
TG6: T33, T43, T46, T48, T62,
T73, T77, T80, T94, T120, T141,
T147, T150, T162, T197
social studies, *TG1:* T6, T23, T24,
T42, T49, T67, T72, T76, T91,
T112, T113, T115, T134, T160,
T181; *TG2:* T6, 33, T113, T124,
T134, T152, T182; *TG3:* T33,
T39, T45, T50, T92, T118,
T131, T190; *TG4:* T7, T18, T25,
T32, T33, T45, T65, T80, T130,
T162, T196; *TG5:* T6, T24, T33,
T41, T45, T58, T70, T93, T125;
TG6: T19, T21, T32, T63, T75,
T95, T117, T131, T146, T163,
T173
technology, *TG2:* T133, T168
visual literacy, *TG1:* T42, T130,
T132, T134, T136, T138, T155,
T156, T159, T164, T166, T168;
TG2: T20, T39, T70, T73, T79,
T111, T131, T138, T139, T158;
TG3: T25, T38, T40, T42, T44,
T46, T48, T51, T117, T118,
T119, T166, T175, T176; *TG4:*
T21, T25, T38, T48, T49, T71,
T72, T75, T77, T81, T122, T148,
T169, T172; *TG5:* T19, T24,
T38, T40, T42, T45, T46, T64,
T69, T137, T160, T161, T164,
T166, T167, T169; *TG6:* T18,
T19, T23, T25, T44, T114, T122,
T123, T137, T138, T142, T169,
T171, T172, T178
See also Centers.

Cue systems. *See* Think About Words.
Cultural diversity. *See also*
Multicultural activities and forms.

D

Decoding skills
cloze. *See* Reading modes.
letter names, *TG1:* T36, T39, T40,
T49, T51, T53, T54, T55, T57,
T87, T128; *TG2:* T50

picture clues, *See* Context; Strategies: Think About Words.

rhyme, *TG1:* T25, T29, T76, T94, T115, T121, T156, T159, T163; *TG2:* T23, **T25,** T54, T59, T85, T115, T166; *TG3:* T84, T127, T134, T137, T141, T150; *TG4:* T27, T61, T68, T79, T84, T91, T127, T134, T152, T159; *TG5:* T56, T160, T172; TG6: T39, T52, T59, T135, T152, T155, T160, T166, T194; *TG6:* T22, T29, T39, T46, T155, T160

See also Phonemic awareness; Phonics; Strategies; Structural analysis.

Details, noting, *TG1:* T19, T28, T45, T46, T49, T50, T82, T109, T118, T156, T166; *TG2:* T23, T24, T28, T29, T86, T114, T128, T135, T136, T144, T162, T172, T178; *TG3:* T17, T42, T63, T171, T178, T180, T186; *TG4:* T21, T29, T47, T75, T86, T92, T114, T124; *TG5:* T17, T26, T86, T87, T117, T120; *TG6:* T16. *See also* Main idea and supporting details.

Diaries and journals. *See* Journal.

Dictionary. *See* My Big Dictionary; My Big Picture Dictionary.

Directions, following, *TG1:* T85, T90, T92; *TG2:* T57, T59, T62, T75, T124, T125; *TG4:* T61, T88, T89, T157, T159

Drafting. *See* Writing skills.

Drama. *See* Creative dramatics.

Drawing conclusions. *See* Conclusions, drawing.

E

Emergent reading. *See* Decoding; Rereading; Responding to literature, options for.

Environmental print, *TG1:* T56; *TG5:* T42, T56, T90; *TG6:* T38, T51, T73, T74

Evaluating literature. *See* Literature, evaluating.

Evaluation. *See* Assessment options, choosing.

Expository text, *TG1:* T14–T33, T60–T79, T126–T139; *TG2:* T34–T63, T126–T153

Extra Support. *See* Individual needs, meeting.

F

Fantasy and realism, *TG2:* T120, T163, T170, T172; *TG3:* T18, T20, T136, T143, T152; *TG5:* T69, T72, T78, T81, T112, T134, T136, T142, T158, T161, T170, T173, T174, T180, T181

Fiction. *See* selections.

Fluency
  oral reading, *TG3:* T84; *TG4:* T84, T152; *TG5:* T86, T188; *TG6:* T28, T90, T192, T195
  reading, *TG3:* T52, T58; *TG5:* T86; *TG6:* T58, T85, T88, T154, T156, T158, T186, T188, T190, T192
  speaking, *TG3:* T30, T158, T188; *TG5:* T86, T152; *TG6:* T92, T128, T194, T200
  writing, *TG3:* T31; *TG6:* T30, T61, T156, T160

Functions of literacy. *see* Literacy, functions of.

G

Genre. *See* Literary genres.

Grammar and usage
  adjectives, *TG2:* T121; *TG4:* T30
  contractions, *TG4:* T70, T73, T74
  nouns, *TG2:* T30; *TG5:* T29; *TG6:* T184
  pronouns, *TG3:* T50, T136; *TG4:* T137, T147, T149, T171, T172, T176; *TG5:* T113, T115, T120, T137, T162, T168; *TG6:* T122
  sentence: beginning, middle, and end, *TG6:* T87, T171
  verbs, *TG5:* T29, T152
  See Language concepts and skills; Speech, parts of.

Graphic information, interpreting
  calendar, *TG1:* T32, T124
  chart, *TG1:* T143; *TG2:* T180; *TG4:*

T94, T98, T126
  diagram, *TG1:* T89
  globe, *TG3:* T190
  graph, *TG1:* T124, T181
  map, *TG2:* T113, T124; *TG3:* T29
  map and globe, *TG5:* T93, T125
  Venn diagram, *TG6:* T154

Graphic organizers
  chart, *TG1:* T26, T112, T116, T135, T146; *TG2:* T21, T50, T57, T125, T148, T153, T180; *TG3:* T30, T31, T46, T50, T61, T63, T82, T125, T128, T188; *TG4:* T17, T46, T94, T98, T126, T131; *TG5:* T55, T90, T112; *TG6:* T31, T52, T82, T94, T154
  graph, *TG2:* T57; *TG4:* T32, T96, T130
  list, *TG1:* T122, T140; *TG2:* T29, T61, T123, T139, T146, T148, T151, T158, T177, T181; *TG4:* T12, T33, T37, T57, T63, T65, T69, T73, T87, T91, T94, T110, T120, T129, T158, T163, T191, T195; *TG5:* T33, T54, T122, T123, T153; *TG6:* T80, T128, T116, T118, T122, T155, T160, T166, T167
  map, *TG2:* T113, T124, T152; *TG3:* T29; *TG4:* T25, T33; *TG6:* T98
  sentence frame, *TG1:* T129
  sentence strip, *TG1:* T57, T89, T174
  story map, *TG6:* T186
  time line, *TG1:* T24, T26; *TG5:* T153
  word map, *TG2:* T88; *TG4:* T62
  word wall, *TG2:* T151; *TG6:* T60, T92, T155
  word web, *TG1:* T31, T63, T177; *TG2:* T129, T157; *TG3:* T37; *TG4:* T30, T160; *TG5:* T37, T63, T159; *TG6:* T30, T92

H

High-Frequency Words, *TG2:* T159, T165, T175, T176; *TG3:* T51, T58, T68, T70, T75, T86, T96, T136, T137, T167, T169, T175, T184, T186; *TG4:* T38, T51, T60, T70, T90, T113, T137, T138, T157, T175, T184, T190; *TG5:* T41, T43, T53, T54, T130, T131, T132, T134,

T137, T149, T161, T163, T178; *TG6*
T39, T40, T47, T58, T69, T70, T71,
T88, T90, T136, T139, T141, T143,
T149, T169, T171, T172, T181,
T190, T192, T200

Home Connection, *TG1:* T17, T25,
T50, T51, T70, T81, T104, T108,
T119, T128, T171, T183; *TG2:* T16,
T27, T30, T55, T109; *TG3:* T16,
T53, T66, T68, T81, T91, T96,
T110, T121, T125, T151, T159,
T179, T184; *TG4:* T16, T55, T85,
T95, T114, T121, T150, T153,
T188; *TG5:* T49, T63, T84, T110,
T119, T128, T145, T159, T173,
T178; *TG6:* T17, T36, T67, T88,
T108, T148, T153, T185, T190,
T200

Home-Community Connections. *See*
Home/Community Connections
Booklet.

Home-school communication. *See*
Home Connections.

Homework. *See* Home connections.

I

Idioms/expressions, *TG1:* T64; *TG2:*
T21; *TG3:* T18, T23, T112, T115,
T118, T122, T149, T166; *TG4:* T19,
T73, T138, T147, T170, T174, T180;
TG5: T19, T40, T65, T72, T164;
TG6: T24, T40, T42, T45, T46, T48,
T49, T51, T70, T75, T119, T143,
T144

Illustrate original writing, *TG1:* T12,
T21, T27, T31, T63, T110, T123,
T147, T153, T179; *TG2:* T31, T37,
T55, T61, T67, T89, T119, T123,
T129, T143, T151, T174, T176,
T180, T181; *TG3:* T18, T27, T37,
T35, T52, T61, T67, T80, T88, T91,
T112, T126, T129, T138, T151,
T165, T167, T180, T190; *TG4:* T31,
T32, T37, T55, T60, T63, T69, T85,
T86, T88, T92, T93, T95, T119,
T129, T195; *TG5:* T27, T36, T37,
T40, T57, T63, T71, T86, T88, T89,
T91, T113, T119, T132, T143, T146,
T150, T153, T154, T173, T174,
T181, T183; *TG6:* T32, T37, T61,

T63, T67, T84, T88, T90, T108,
T128, T129, T135, T156, T161,
T167, T193, T195

Illustrator's craft, *TG3:* T17, T25, T38;
TG5: T26, T46, T66, T118

Illustrators of selections. *See*
Selections.

Independent reading, *TG1:* T37, T86,
T87, T102, T176; *TG2:* T86, T87,
T111, T142, T170, T178, T179; *TG3:*
T31, T52, T86, T89, T124, T150,
T154, T155, T178, T184, T187;
TG4: T92, T93, T192, T193; *TG5:*
T48, T80, T118, T144, T172, T180;
TG6: T82, T90, T152, T184, T192

Independent writing, *TG1:* T87, T177;
TG2: T87, T179; *TG3:* T52, T89,
T152, T187, T1899; *TG4:* T93,
T193; *TG5:* T89, T181; *TG6:* T90,
T91

Individual needs, meeting
challenge, *TG1:* T10, T19, T28,
T29, T33, T42, T51, T52, T59,
T65, T67, T77, T82, T84, T102,
T109, T121, T124, T135, T138,
T144, T147, T148, T157, T160,
T175, T180; *TG2:* T10, T31,
T32, T41, T53, T57, T60, T69,
T88, T89, T111, T121, T123,
T139, T148, T169, T177, T183;
TG3: T10, T22, T24, T26, T30,
T32, T40, T41, T46, T56, T70,
T76, T82, T84, T92, T104,
T119, T121, T128, T129, T141,
T152, T154, T158, T168, T175,
T182, T188, T189; *TG4:* T10,
T26, T28, T32, T33, T58, T60,
T62, T63, T65, T80, T88, T91,
T95, T96, T108, T119, T120,
T124, T127, T129, T143, T156,
T161, T162, T173, T177, T180,
T185; *TG5:* T10, T20, T21, T29,
T33, T46, T50, T59, T67, T72,
T75, T82, T104, T112, T118,
T123, T125, T138, T145, T153,
T155, T167, T182, T184; *TG6:*
T10, T22, T27, T29, T30, T43,
T44, T49, T56, T59, T62, T86,
T88, T93, T106, T120, T138,
T157, T173, T175, T177, T179,
T180, T181, T188, T194

extra support, *TG1:* T10, T16, T18,
T20, T23, T28, T32, T38, T40,
T46, T52, T53, T54, T57, T64,
T68, T82, T83, T84, T102,
T111, T113, T114, T116, T121,
T140, T142, T144, T163, T164,
T172, T173, T174; *TG2:* T10,
T19, T23, T28, T29, T40, T54,
T56, T58, T60, T68, T80, T82,
T83, T84, T110, T121, T131,
T132, T136, T138, T144, T146,
T163, T164, T166, T168, T172,
T175; *TG3:* T10, T19, T20, T21,
T25, T26, T28, T29, T48, T50,
T51, T52, T54, T55, T57, T58,
T69, T71, T75, T80, T82, T83,
T84, T85, T104, T113, T116,
T122, T124, T126, T127, T130,
T136, T139, T144, T150, T152,
T153, T154, T155, T156, T166,
T169, T180, T181, T183, T184,
T188; *TG4:* T10, T19, T20, T26,
T28, T29, T38, T39, T41, T47,
T56, T57, T58, T59, T60, T63,
T73, T86, T87, T88, T89, T90,
T94, T108, T117, T126, T127,
T128, T137, T148, T154, T155,
T156, T157, T158, T161, T168,
T170, T171, T174, T179, T182,
T186, T187, T189, T190; *TG5:*
T10, T18, T24, T28, T29, T30,
T38, T50, T51, T52, T53, T54,
T56, T71, T74, T78, T82, T83,
T85, T104, T113, T114, T115,
T120, T121, T136, T137, T139,
T146, T147, T148, T150, T160,
T161, T162, T163, T165, T168,
T174, T175, T178; *TG6:* T10,
T18, T23, T24, T28, T29, T33,
T41, T42, T50, T54, T55, T56,
T57, T58, T69, T70, T72, T77,
T78, T79, T84, T85, T87, T88,
T106, T115, T126, T127, T136,
T140, T154, T155, T156, T158,
T162, T168, T170, T171, T174,
T186, T187, T188
students acquiring English. *See*
Students Acquiring English.

Inferences, making
about characters' actions and feelings, *TG1:* T113; *TG2:* T24,
T68, T73, T78, T112; *TG3:* T17,

T24, T25, T26, T27, T42, T81, T111, T113, T114, T120, T125, T126, T128, T180, T194; *TG4:* T27, T44, T55, T176; *TG5:* T17, T18, T23, T24, T27, T28, T30, T42, T47, T50, T70, T82, T112, T119, T122, T159, T173; *TG6:* T19, T26, T28, T43, T44, T53, T122, T124, T126, T184, T185

by drawing conclusions, *TG1:* **T167, T172;** *TG3:* T25, T28, T74, T114; *TG4:* **T21, T36,** T40, T44; *TG6:* T44, T62, T69, T125, T126

by predicting, *TG1:* T74, **T113;** *TG2:* T18, T24, T38, T68, T72, T78, T110, T114, T130; *TG3:* T36, T38, **T39, T54,** T66, T88, T110, T112, T134, T164, T186; *TG4:* T44, T150, T168, T170, T176; *TG5:* T16, T18, T22, T36, T38, T42, T62, T64, T70, T88, T110, T112, T128; *TG6:* T18, T128, T185

from illustrations, *TG3:* T17, T25, T36, T38, T54, T74, T78, T111, T142, T143; *TG5:* T16, T36, T120, T131, T132, T161, T166

Interactive Learning
building background, *TG1:* **T16, T36, T62, T108, T128, T152;** *TG3:* **T16, T36, T164; TG5: T36, T63, T128, T158;** *TG6:* **T16, T36, T66, T112, T166**

independent reading and writing, *TG1:* **T86–T87, T176–T177;** *TG2:* **T86–T87, T178–T179;** *TG3:* **T88–T89, T186–T187;** *TG4:* **T92, T93, T192, T193;** *TG5:* **T88–T89, T180–T181;** *TG6:* **T90-T91, T192-T193**

shared reading and writing, *TG1:* **T36-T37, T62-T63, T128-T129, T152-T153;** *TG2:* **T36–T37, T66–T67, T128–T129, T156–T157;** *TG3:* **T36–T37, T66–T67, T134–T135, T164–T165;** *TG4:* **T36, T68, T134, T166;** *TG5:* **T36–T37, T62-T63, T128–T129, T158–T159;** *TG6:* **T36–T37, T66–T67, T134-T135, T166-T167**

theme, launching the, *TG1:* **T12, T104;** *TG2:* **T12, T104;** *TG3:* **T12, T106;** *TG4:* **T12, T110;** *TG5:* **T12, T106;** *TG6:* **T12, T108**

Invented spelling. *See* Spelling, temporary.

/p/, *TG3:* T19, T29, T74, T119; *TG4:* **T73,** T77, T78, **T87, T143;** *TG5:* T19, T135, T139, T144, T148, T168, T176; *TG6:* T29, T37, T49, T55, T67, T76, T115, T117, T143, T188

/r/, *TG3:* T119; *TG6:* **T79,** T85, T86, T116, T149, T151

/s/, *TG2:* **T161, T173, T174;** *TG3:* T19, T22, T29, T41, T56, T87, T144, T155, T165, T172, T181; *TG4:* **T136;** *TG5:* T29, T45, T85, T149 *TG6:* T29, T37, T49, T55, T67, T116, T127, T145, T188

/t/, *TG3:* T29, T119, T127; *TG5:* **T75,** T83, T84, T85, T148, T164; *TG6:* T21, T29, T37, T44, T55, T67, T127, T168

/w/, *TG5:* **T133,** T144, T147, T151; *TG6:* T29, T37, T49, T55, T56, T67, **T77,** T117, T148, T169

/y/, *TG6:* **T139,** T141, T154, T155, T187, T188

/z/, **TG5:** T164

phonograms

-and, *TG5:* **T45, T52;** *TG6:* T37, T67, T188

-at, *TG3:* **T77, T84;** *TG6:* T29, T37, T67, T127, T188

-et, *TG6:* T37, **T49,** T54, T55, T67, T90, T188

-ig, *TG4:* **T79, T88;** *TG6:* T29

-it, *TG4:* **T139, T156;** *TG5:* **T79;** *TG6:* T37, T67, T188

-ot, *TG5:* **T139, T148, T176;** *TG6:* T37, T67, T117, T188

-ug, *TG3:* **T141, T154,** T186; *TG6:* T37, T67, T188

-ut, *TG6:* **T151,** T156, T188, T192

See Decoding skills; Strategies: Think About Words; Structural Analysis.

Phonograms. *See* Phonics: phonograms.

Plot. *See* Story elements/story structure.

Pluralism. *See* Cultural diversity.

Poems in Teacher's Edition

"Bear Cub's Day," T110

"City Streets," *TG6:* T16

"First Snow," *TG4:* T166

"Five Little Ducks," *TG3:* T36, T57, T58

"I Love Little Pussy," T66

"I'm Glad the Sky Is Painted Blue," *TG1:* T121, T123

"In a Dark, Dark Wood," *TG6:* T166

"In Downtown Philadelphia," *TG4:* T134, T157

"Just Watch," T36

"Maxie and the Taxi," *TG6:* T36

"Mix a Pancake," *TG6:* T112

"My Bird is Small," *TG4:* T114

"My Family," *TG2:* T156

"My Teddy Bear," *TG3:* T134, T155

"Night Comes . . .," T110

"Others Are Special," *TG2:* T108

"Preferred Vehicles," *TG6:* T66

"Pussycat, Pussycat," *TG6:* T134

"Rain Song," T128

"Reflection," T62

"Roses Are Red," T152

"Somersaults," *TG5:* T62, T85

"The Teddy Bears' Picnic," *TG5:* T158, T185

"Teddy Bear, Teddy Bear," *TG5:* T21

"Travel Plans," *TG2:* T128, T147

"Twinkle, Twinkle, Little Star," *TG1:* T121

"What Is Pink?" *TG1:* T104, T121, T173

"When All the World's Asleep," *TG3:* T164, T183

"Whistling," *TG5:* T16, T29

"With a Friend," *TG4:* T36

"Yesterday's Newspaper," *TG2:* T36

Poetry

introducing, reading, responding to, *TG1:* T62, T104, T121, T123, T128, T152, T184; *TG2:* T36, T108, T128, T156; *TG3:* T36, T46, T57, T66, T108, T110, T134, T155; *TG4:* T36, T114, T134, T157, T166; *TG5:* T16, T29, T36, T62, T110, T21, T158; *TG6:* T16, T36, T66, T112, T134, T166

Predictions, making,

from previewing, *TG1:* T16, T38, T62, T108, T152; *TG2:* T16, T18, T36, T38, T66, T68, T86, T108, T110, T128, T130, T156, T172, T178; *TG3:* T16, T26, T66, T110, T134, T164; *TG4:* T16, T36, T93, T114, T134, T166, T192; *TG5:* T16, T36, T62, T110, T128, T158; *TG6:* T16, T36, T66, T90, T112, T134, T166, T192

while reading, *TG1:* T18, T43, T64, T74, T108, T152; *TG2:* T17, T24, T40, T43, T72, T78, T114; *TG3:* T38, **T39, T54,** T66, T88, T112, T136, T186; *TG4:* T44, T150, T170, T176; *TG5:* T18, T22, T38, T42, T64, T70, T88, T112, T180; *TG6:* T112, T166

Previewing

book covers, *TG2:* T16, T36, T66, T86, T108, T128, T152, T156, T178; **TG3:** T16, T36, T66, T88, T110, T134, T164, T186; *TG4:* T16, T68, T93, T114, T134, T166, T192; *TG5:* T16, T36, T62, T88, T110, T120, T128, T158, T180

illustrations, *TG1:* T36, T86, T152; *TG2:* T16, T36, T66, T86, T108, T128, T152, T156, T178; *TG3:* T36, T88, T110, T134, T164, T186; *TG4:* T16, T36, T68, T93, T114, T134, T166, T192; *TG5:* T16, T36, T62, T88, T110, T120, T128, T158; *TG6:* T36, T84, T90, T112, T134, T166, T192

photos, *TG6:* T66

text, *TG3:* T88, T110, T164, T186; *TG5:* T16

title, *TG1:* T16, T36, T62, T86, T108, T128, T152; *TG2:* T16, T36, T66, T86, T108, T128, T152, T156, T178; *TG3:* T16, T36, T66, T88, T110, T134, T164, T186; *TG4:* T16, T36, T68, T93, T114, T134, T166, T192; *TG5:* T16, T36, T62, T88, T110, T120, T128, T158, T180; *TG6:* T16, T36, T84, T90, T112,

T176; *TG4:* T24, T52, T82, T122, T142, T150, T182; *TG5:* T24, T46, T78, T94, T142, T170; *TG6:* T24, T50, T80

reflecting, *TG1:* T92, T182; *TG2:* T92, T184; *TG3:* T94, T192; *TG4:* T98, T198; *TG5:* T94, T186; *TG6:* T97, T198

theme goals, *TG1:* T94, T184; *TG2:* T94; *TG3:* T96, T194; *TG4:* T98, T200; *TG5:* T96, T188; *TG6:* T98, T200

Sequence of events, *TG1:* T22, T43, T139, T142; *TG2:* T23, T43, T56; *TG3:* T17, T118, T124; *TG4:* T26, T45, T50, T56, T124, T153, T181, T186; *TG6:* T17, T43, T54, T113, T160

Setting. *See* Story elements.

Shapes
circles, *TG2:* T36, T37, T55, T63
square, *TG2:* T37, T63
triangle, *TG2:* T37, T63; *TG4:* T41

Shared learning. *See* Cooperative learning activities.

Shared reading. *See* Reading modes, shared reading.

Shared reading and writing. *See* Interactive Learning.

Shared writing. *See* Writing, shared.

Skills. *See* Categorizing; Cause-effect; Conclusions, drawing; Decoding skills; Details, noting; Fantasy and realism; Interactive Learning; Main ideas; Minilessons; Phonics; Predicting outcomes; Sequence of events; Story elements/story structure; Strategies, reading; Study skills.

Social studies activities. *See* Cross-curricular activities.

Songs in Teacher's Book
"ABC Song," *TG1:* T36, H11
"The Bear Went Over the Mountain," *TG5:* T12, H10
"Eensy Weensy Spider," *TG3:* T16, H11
"Five Little Ducks," *TG3:* T36, T58, H12
"I Am Special, I Am Me," *TG1:*

T12, T29, T94, H12
"If You're Happy and You Know It," *TG1:* T16, H10
"Japanese Rain Song," *TG1:* T145
"John Jacob Jingleheimer Schmidt," *TG2:* T12, H10
"Make New Friends," *TG4:* T12, H10
"Mary Had a Little Lamb," *TG4:* T110, H13
"The More We Get Together," *TG4:* T68, H12
"Oh Where Oh Where Has My Little Dog Gone?" *TG4:* T16, H11
"Old MacDonald Had a Farm," *TG2:* T32; *TG3:* T12, H10
"Punchinello," *TG5:* T12, H10
"Row, Row, Row Your Boat," *TG2:* T16, H11
"Sing a Rainbow," *TG1:* T108, H13–H14
"Sing a Song of Sixpence," *TG6:* T108, H11
"Twinkle, Twinkle, Little Star," *TG3:* T106, T127, H13
"Ways to Go!" *TG6:* T12, H10
"What Shall We Do When We All Go Out?" *TG4:* T64
"Where Is Thumpkin?" *TG2:* T62

Sound-spelling patterns. *See* Phonics; Spelling.

Speaking activities
form
choral speaking, *TG1:* T17, T32, T145, T170; *TG4:* T54
description, *TG1:* T28, T38, T51, T56, T62, T111, T113, T122, T129, T178, T181; *TG2:* T28, T31, T40, T56, T80, T120, T150; *TG3:* T17, T60; *TG4:* T44, T45, T72, T76, T92, T128, T130, T160, T194; *TG5:* T36, T47, T57, T62, T67, T86, T87, T118
dictation, *TG1:* T21, T27, T31, T81, T120, T123, T129, T132, T147, T170; *TG3:* T30, T57; *TG4:* T12, T135, T153, T167, T195; *TG5:* T16, T27, T31, T57, T63, T119; *TG6:* T32, T83, T84, T91,

T93, T129, T153, T161, T167

discussion, *TG1:* T18, T23, T24, T27, T30, T38, T56, T66, T91, T108, T112, T122, T130, T132, T160, T171, T181; *TG2:* T16, T19, T21, T24, T266, T27, T30, T33, T36, T38, T52, T59, T60, T63, T68, T71, T82, T86, T90, T104, T112, T122, T124, T128, T130, T132, T136, T140, T141, T148, T149, T150, T156, T158, T160, T166, T180, T182, T186; *TG3:* T30, T85, T92, T130, T134, T188; *TG4:* T16, T18, T19, T20, T21, T23, T27, T31, T33, T38, T40, T44, T46, T48, T50, T52, T62, T68, T75, T78, T85, T87, T90, T95, T98, T110, T114, T116, T121, T130, T136, T142, T146, T147, T148, T150, T155, T163, T166, T180, T182, T195; *TG5:* T64, T83, T122; *TG6:* T12, T27, T32, T36, T43, T92, T197

dramatics, *TG1:* T17, T22, T26, T32, T86, T87, T88; *TG2:* T16, T19, T22, T26, T30, T33, T48, T49, T77, T81, T82, T91, T119, T132, T150, T171, T177; *TG3:* T21, T27, T28, T33, T80, T88, T124, T148, T151, T157, T185; *TG4:* T18, T26, T27, T33, T42, T71, T119, T125, T147, T153, T160, T178, T192; *TG5:* T21, T27, T30, T47, T49, T119, T122, T145, T173, T179; *TG6:* T16, T17, T26, T27, T28, T30, T32, T43, T56, T60, T113, T125, T126, T153, T185, T192, T200

explanation, *TG1:* T33, T72, T91, T94, T166, T167; *TG2:* T22; *TG4:* T21, T25, T27, T40, T41, T48, T62, T180, T194; *TG5:* T55

introduction, *TG1:* T81; *TG4:* T30, T128

T

U

V

W